Books should be returned or renewed by the last date above. Renew by phone **03000 41 31 31** or online *www.kent.gov.uk/libs*

Libraries Registration & Archives

C333913308

the ACHIEVEMENT HABIT

the ACHIEVEMENT HABIT

STOP WISHING, START DOING, *and* TAKE COMMAND OF YOUR LIFE

BERNARD ROTH

HARPER
BUSINESS

An Imprint of HarperCollins*Publishers*

HarperCollins books may be purchased for educational, business, or sales
promotional use. For information, please e-mail the Special Markets Department at SPsales@harpercollins.com.

Illustrations on pages 82 and 83 by Rolf Faste
Illustration on page 92 by David Kelley
All other illustrations by Thomas Both

FIRST EDITION

Designed by Renato Stanisic

Library of Congress Cataloging-in-Publication Data has been applied for.

ISBN: 978-0-06-235610-9

15 16 17 18 19 OV/RRD 10 9 8 7 6 5

TO THE MEMORY OF ROLF FASTE AND BILL MOGGRIDGE

CONTENTS

the
ACHIEVEMENT
HABIT

INTRODUCTION: YELLOW-EYED CATS

Paddy's idea wasn't the most daring in the class.

When you first met him, you could tell he came from a military background. It was evident in his stance—stoic and somewhat intimidating. He went to boarding school in Northern Ireland from age seven to eighteen and then joined the Royal Marines, where he served for ten years.

Civilian life scared him, and after leaving the military, he quickly sought out the safety net of a job within a large corporation and a regimented schedule. A journalist, he moved around the world quite a bit, finding work at places like the BBC and CNBC. "I'm something of a company man," he would later tell me.

When I met him he was at Stanford University on a one-year fellowship for midcareer journalists. He was taking a class of mine, "The Designer in Society," which encourages students to examine and take control of their lives. I've been a professor of engineering at Stanford for fifty-two years, and along the way I've met too many engineers who once dreamed of starting a company of their own—and instead ended up working for large Silicon Valley companies and never taking that big step toward making their dreams a reality. Only a small percentage ever followed through on what they really wanted to do with their lives, and I hoped to do something to change that. Having talent and good ideas is only part of the equation. The next step—the harder step—is the *doing*, taking the responsibility for designing success in your own life.

In 1969 I created my "Designer in Society" class as a way to encourage students to think differently about how they achieve goals in their lives—to get them to stop thinking wistfully about possibilities and start actually *doing*.[1] In developing the course, I employed principles that we now call "design thinking" (a big concept we'll get into a bit later) as well as a series of ideas and exercises I've found to be useful in assisting people to break through walls that are mostly of their own making.

At the heart of the course is a self-selected term project: students must either do something they have wanted to do but never done, or handle something that is a problem in their lives. I am available to discuss their choices. I emphasize that it is their project, however, and that they are doing it for themselves, not for me. Ultimately they decide which projects to work on. I don't decide whether they're good enough or big enough, and I don't grade on anything other than whether they do what they set out to do. If they finish, they pass. If they don't, they don't get credit.

One of the most important lessons students take away from the class is to be honest with themselves—really deep-down honest. The more self-aware you can become, the happier you can be; by better understanding your motivations and identity, you can figure out how to design your life to be more satisfying and fulfilling.

Paddy dug deep and came to the realization that although he had thrived in every institution he was part of, he had never been really happy. That was in part because he had a very conflicted relationship with authority and the large media organization he belonged to. He had sought it out because it was what he knew, yet he also resented and rebelled against it because he wanted something more personally satisfying. Once he realized and acknowledged this fact, he was able to use that knowledge.

For his project, Paddy decided to produce his own radio show.

When he compared his idea to others', he wasn't sure it stacked up very well. After all, we had students doing things that seemed on the surface much more exciting (one student was going to hurl himself out of an airplane!), creative (building a rocket), or ambitious (students turning their bodies into machines to prepare for their first triathlons).

For Paddy a radio show was a major undertaking, and it took him a while to realize why he was so drawn to it. He had been a radio reporter, but never a producer. For the first time in his life he would be making something from his own ideas, without oversight. It *was* a daring choice for him, akin to starting his own business.

I NOW TEACH MY class at one of the world's leading centers for innovation, the Hasso Plattner Institute of Design at Stanford, commonly called the d.school, where I am the academic director and one of the founders. It's gotten pretty famous—the *Wall Street Journal* called it "the hottest graduate program," and we have more students signing up for our classes than we have seats for them.[2] The d.school is not linked to any particular department but instead brings together students and faculty from many disciplines to create an environment that fosters creativity, innovation, and collaboration.

What the d.school does for students is open up their worlds, challenging their "automatic" thinking and assumptions and showing them the vast multitude of possibilities around them. We write on whiteboards, Post-it notes, and napkins. We try things. We fail. We try again. We fail better. We get things right in ways we might never have imagined, and we gain a better understanding about ourselves and others in the process.

Many who have taken my course over the years credit it with helping them achieve significant personal and professional successes in their lives, and I have gone on to conduct workshops throughout the world based on the concepts taught in the class. It's empowering to realize you have more control than you ever knew over what you achieve in life. When you are not happy with an aspect of your life, you can change it! Really, you can.

In my class students have designed and built musical instruments, furniture, vehicles, and clothing. They've written books, poetry, and music. They've flown and jumped out of various aircraft, done stand-up comedy, and driven racing cars. They've learned how to cook, weld, tend bar, speak new languages, and save lives. They've repaired relationships with parents, siblings, and friends. They've run marathons, lost weight, and braved the wilderness.

One of the most inspiring projects I watched unfold was that of a student named Joel who reconciled with his father two months before his father died unexpectedly of an aortic aneurysm. Thirty years later I still feel tears of joy well up in my eyes whenever I run into Joel, his wife, or his children.

The father of another student, Cyndie, had always prohibited her from riding a motorcycle because he'd suffered a terrible accident when he was younger. Naturally, Cyndie wanted to learn to ride one. She decided to buy a motorcycle and learn to drive it as her project. Several months after my class, Bill, one of her former drawing instructors, was standing in front of his design office in Palo Alto when she rode up on her motorcycle and asked if he would like to go for a ride. He got on, thinking she meant around the block. Forty-five minutes later they arrived at the beach. That was twenty-eight years ago. They now have three grown children together.

Another woman in my class overcame her fear of water and learned to swim. I ran into her some months later and she told me she was learning Italian, having felt empowered by her first endeavor in my class. A few years after that she earned special training certificates that enabled her to change her career field—all thanks to the momentum and inspiration gained from developing her achievement habit.

What she and other students demonstrate not only in class but also in their lives after graduation is that achievement *can* be learned. It is a muscle, and once you learn to flex it, there's no end to what you can accomplish in life.

One of my favorite things to do with a group is to ask people to think about who stops them from accomplishing the things they want. It's always entertaining to listen to them explain how their parents, spouses, children, colleagues, bosses—you name it—prevent them from reaching their goals. These perceived obstacles are simply excuses; in almost every case, when you really dig down, it's you who are sabotaging yourself.

Yes, sometimes there are real external obstacles, and most people don't realize that they have the power to overcome them.

I once interviewed a job applicant who told me of her encounter with pirates when she and her boyfriend were sailing around the world. While the boat was anchored off the coast of Indonesia, she was sunbathing while he went into town. Suddenly she heard a noise and saw heavily armed men boarding their boat. They pointed guns at her and demanded money. Vulnerable and alone, with no money to give them, she kept her composure and was able to convince them that the powdered milk she had on board was a worthy replacement for cash. She appealed to their parental instincts, knowing milk was hard to come by and that they probably desperately needed some for their children. They accepted the milk with gratitude and left her and the boat unharmed. After hearing her unique solution and admiring her clearheadedness, I hired her on the spot.

That said, most of the time there are no pirates. We simply stop ourselves.

To demonstrate this in my class, I ask for a volunteer to come to the front of the room. When he is standing in front of me, I hold out a water bottle (or other object) and say, "Please try to take it away from me." The volunteer will tug at the bottle—at first tentatively, because I'm older and look weaker, and then more forcefully when he realizes I have it firmly in my grasp. Eventually I ask the student to stop trying.

I then ask him to listen carefully to my next instruction. This time I say, "Please *take* the bottle from me." What follows is essentially the same action as before, with more force and maybe some twisting added. Sometimes he'll decide to change tactics and ask me to hand it over. I always refuse.

Finally I ask him, "Do you have a younger sibling or cousin?" I then ask the student to imagine that I am that person, we're both kids, and there are no parents around. Furthermore, I tell him to imagine the situation has gotten very annoying, and it is time for him to reclaim the bottle from me. Then I repeat the instruction, "*Take* the bottle from me."

Participants who get what I'm driving at simply whisk the object out of my hand, leaving me no time to resist. I am overpowered by their intention to take the object. They have manifested a dynamic, elegant flow of intention to *do*, which is in sharp contrast to their previous static, tentative *attempt* at doing. Even better, in taking the object they usually actually exert less force than they did before.

I use this exercise to show that when you *do*, you are using *power*; when you *try*, you are using *force*. In life, if you want to get things done, it is much better to be powerful than to be forceful.

Of course the switch isn't so easy to make in real life. We've all had the experience of making up our minds to do something and then not doing it—New Year's resolutions, exercise, fidelity, deadlines, and work habits being just a few examples. In order to make the switch we must understand our behavior. The classic model (and popular wisdom) says that we think things through first and then act on our thoughts. Interestingly, this does not hold up in clinical testing.

By decoding local patterns of MRI signals in various brain regions, clinicians have shown that the brain can send motor signals for actions *before* the brain consciously forms the actual thoughts that account for the actions. You do what you do, and then you make up the reason for doing it. Most of our action is more the result of habit than reasoning. So that leads to a question: How do you bridge the gap between trying and doing, between talking about something and acting on it, and ultimately between failure and success?

In this book you'll find stories, advice, and exercises designed to help you create a different experience in your life—experience being the real teacher. When we established the d. school at Stanford, we were determined to create experiences where students deal with real people, solve real problems, and make a difference. The results have been hugely gratifying. The students have gained a sense of purpose, mastery, and intrinsic motivation. A magical thing happens: the grade is no longer a useful or meaningful motivator. Intrinsic motivation has taken over, and the work is its own reward.

By the end of the book, as a reader you will understand:

- Why *trying* is not good enough and how it is very different from *doing*.
- Why excuses, even legitimate ones, are self-defeating.
- How to change your self-image into one of a doer and achiever, and why this is important.
- How subtle language changes can resolve existential dilemmas and also barriers to action.
- How to build resiliency by reinforcing what you do (your action) rather than what you accomplish, so you can easily recover from temporary setbacks.
- How to train yourself to ignore distractions that prevent you from achieving your goals.
- How to be open to learning from your own experience and that of others.

The mind is trickier than we think and is always working with our egos to sabotage our best intentions. That's the human condition. What we have going for us is that, if we choose to, we can be mindful about controlling our intentions to create habits that make our lives better.

The ideas in this book are rooted in the design thinking tradition. Whereas others have applied its tenets in organizational innovation and change,[3] I have chosen to focus on personal transformation and empowerment. Stanford's d.school is a pioneer in the design thinking movement, and as one of its founders I have witnessed intense interest from all sectors of education, industry, and government.

A wonderful book called *The Adjusted American*, a now somewhat outdated sociology text, attempts to explain the everyday neuroses of the average American.[4] In it is a great story about the authors' three-year-old son. The boy had known only two cats, both Siamese, a breed with blue eyes. One day a Persian cat appeared and the boy squatted down on the sidewalk for a better look. Suddenly he jumped up and ran into the house, shouting, "I saw a cat with yellow eyes, Mommy! A cat with yellow eyes!"

Encountering a different breed of cat forever changed a small piece of this child's worldview. In the same way, we don't realize how many of our fixed views of the world are based on limited samples of reality. It is my hope that this book will bring yellow-eyed cats into your world.

YELLOW-EYED CATS WERE BROUGHT into Paddy's world. Until the class, he had not thought of himself as an innovator or creator. He was achieving in the more commonly accepted sense—that is, he had become an officer in the marines and he was doing well as a journalist—but he had not had any breakthrough *personal* achievements that were of his own making. He was just doing a good job walking the paths others had created. In my class he learned not to recoil or procrastinate when a new idea arose, but to act. Just that small insight, which we call bias toward action (which we'll discuss later), has changed his worldview and pushed him down several roads in the last two years. He prototyped and produced several new products for the radio program *Marketplace*, published a book about economics (*Man vs. Markets*), completed a previously abandoned novel, and started on the road to building his own business.

Today, three years after leaving the d.school, Paddy is making another gut-wrenching leap, from the safety of being an employee to the wide-open space of being his own boss. Part of him is screaming in terror at this idea, and the part that channels what he learned in the class is telling him to go one small step at a time, to prototype his ideas, and to trust the design thinking process and himself.

You can do the same thing. As you read on, you will find out how you can become more effective at solving problems, more focused on things that matter, and more satisfied with your life. This book will open your eyes to the power you have to change your life for the better. It will give you confidence to finally do things you have always wanted to do while ridding yourself of issues that stand in the way of your full potential. And the *experience* of taking control of your life will change your reality, making it possible to achieve almost anything you seriously want to do.

A NOTE ABOUT DESIGN THINKING

So what is this design thinking stuff, anyway?

Design thinking is a set of general practices a group of us has developed over the years that are effective in solving design challenges. A design challenge can apply to just about any kind of product or experience. It's not just about how to build a better mousetrap (though that's part of it); it's also about things that are not physical objects: how to improve the wait time at a popular amusement park, how to clean up a highway, how to more efficiently get food to needy people, how to improve online dating, and so on.

Design thinking is an amorphous concept that was given its name by David Kelley, another Stanford professor and co-founder of IDEO, when he was trying to explain that successful designers have a different mind-set and approach from most people. We all adopted and adapted it at the d.school, and the idea took off like a shot. Suddenly everyone was talking about this new concept, design thinking, something I'd been practicing for half a century without having a proper name for it.

It's difficult to give an exact definition for design thinking, however, but because I'm one of its "inventors" I can certainly give you an idea of the principles, which we'll get into throughout the book:

1. Empathize. This is where it starts. When you design, you're not primarily doing it for yourself; you're doing it with other people's needs and desires in mind. Whether you're designing a better roller coaster or a better hospital

waiting room experience, the idea is to care about the users' experiences and figure out how to help. In this step you're learning what the issues are.

2. Define the problem.[5] Narrow down which problem you're going to solve or which question you're going to answer.

3. Ideate. Generate possible solutions using any means you like—brainstorming, mind mapping, sketching on napkins . . . however you work best.

4. Prototype. Without going crazy to make anything perfect (or even close to it), build your project in physical form, or develop the plans for what you're going to enact.

5. Test and get feedback.

Though I've just given you a list of principles, it rarely works that neatly or follows that specific order. You may get to step 4 and realize you need to go back to step 2, or repeat step 3 several times. That's built into the process; one of the other important concepts of design thinking is that failure can be a valuable part of the process. "The only thing to fear is fear itself," said Franklin D. Roosevelt, and I say the only thing to fear is not learning from your mistakes. You can fail lots of times as long as you learn from these failures and figure a solution out in the end.

We also focus on action—*doing* rather than overthinking. In one of our classes, "Launchpad," professors lead you through starting your own company in ten weeks, and by the end of that time you'll be producing income. Or you can go to a conventional business school and spend a year plotting and planning before taking an actual step.

Design thinking is very group-focused. We practice radical collaboration—both as professors and as students.

What's different about my work and this book is that design thinking is normally applied *outward*—toward building solutions for other people's problems in a business or school setting. My special interest is in using it toward improving your own life and interpersonal relationships, designing the best version of yourself.

While much of my teaching is rooted in this framework, not all of it is. There are many exercises throughout the book that you can try on for size. My view is that you take what's useful to you and spin it in whatever direction works. Sometimes I'll think someone has done an exercise "wrong," only to find out that he got more out of it than I'd even anticipated. I'm a big fan of whatever works.

It is in this spirit that I say, Let's get started.

NOTHING
is what you think it is

CHAPTER 1

How can I tell what I think till I see what I say?

—E. M. Forster

Your life has no meaning.

I'm not telling you this to make you think about jumping off the nearest bridge; instead I mean it in a much more contemplative way. Let's first acknowledge that the meaning we find in people, objects, and our own circumstances is subjective. These things have no inherent meaning. Functional and dysfunctional behavior both result from choices people make based on meanings they create. This also means that we have the power to alter our perceptions, revising perceptions that bring us down and enhancing those that help us. Your outlook on life is deeply entwined in your propensity for success. Miserable blowhards can achieve, however they still wind up miserable. That's not success. Success is doing what you love *and* being happy about it.

To learn how to get a better handle on your perceptions, emotions, and behavior, it is useful to look at how you think.

YOU GIVE EVERYTHING ITS MEANING

Mike, a graduate student in my class at Stanford University, planned to design a musical instrument for that summer's Burning Man festival as his project. The festival is held each year the week before Labor Day in the Black Rock Desert in Nevada; among the main attractions at Burning Man are massive art pieces, machines, and structures created by the participants. Mike got the idea of doing his project in my class because we both attend the festival. Mike wanted to construct a wearable pipe organ powered in a most unusual way: it would contain a small fire-powered boiler that would then provide steam that could be directed through different pipes to produce music.

The project seemed overly ambitious to me, yet I did not discourage Mike because he appeared highly motivated. Our agreement was that he would come to see me once a week and report on his progress.

Things didn't go according to plan. At first he visited me sporadically with excuses and little progress to show, and I soon tired of wasting time for both of us on these meetings. I told Mike to forget about the meetings unless he needed me for some reason; I would wait to see the final result.

When the festival arrived, I went at a prearranged time to Mike's campsite at Burning Man. I brought along Adrian and Steve, two very capable engineers who were part of my Burning Man group and who had a keen interest in seeing the final product. Mike's presentation was a disaster. Clearly he had not finished, and during his demonstration the instrument worked badly or not at all. Mike was embarrassed, I was embarrassed, and Adrian and Steve were embarrassed for him. Had I been asked to evaluate Mike for a job at that moment I would not have been able to recommend him in good conscience.

Fast-forward three years. I was again at Burning Man with Adrian and Steve, watching a dance performance by a group called the Flaming Lotus Girls, done in conjunction with an amazing animated sculpture called *Serpent Mother*, a 168-foot-long metallic sculpture of a skeletal serpent coiled around her egg. Propane fire ran down her spine from forty-one flamethrowers that erupted from the top of her vertebrae and shot flames twenty feet in the air. Her head and jaws were hydraulically operated. The three of us stood there transfixed, as did thousands of other participants. Everyone agreed it was by far the most impressive project at the festival. We watched for a while and then wandered off.

A few hours later I returned by myself. By this time the dancers were gone, and the crowd had thinned. I was able to get up close to look at the details of *Serpent Mother*'s construction. The mechanical engineer in me became curious about the joints connecting the movable head, and I asked one of the attendants about its structure. He told me he didn't know, but "that guy over there holding the controller knows everything." I looked up, and there was Mike. I walked over to him, and without hesitation we hugged and started to talk.

It turned out he was very active in the Flaming Lotus Girls organization and their mission to bring more women into the maker culture that stands at the intersection of sculpture, kinetics, robotics, pyrotechnics, and electronic technology; they use a collaborative process that empowers participants to learn new skills and become active artists. Obviously I was very impressed by what he had accomplished.

On my eight-hour drive home after the festival I had plenty of time to think about my experience. I remembered how embarrassed I had felt for Mike about his class project, and thought of how proud I was now of his new endeavor. Based on my previous experience, I did not have a high opinion of his abilities; yet, if anyone asked me now, I would not hesitate to give him a strong recommendation. Clearly Mike was not who I had thought he was, and his story certainly was much more nuanced and complex than I'd imagined.

"Did I redeem myself?" he wrote to me afterward, and I had to laugh. Yes, he did.

Getting to know someone can take somewhere around forever. People are always changing and evolving for both good and bad, and we are all capable of reinvention. I don't know what Mike had going on in his life during my class. My guess is that he was just a typical student who procrastinated and didn't place enough value on his schoolwork. At the time, that's all he was to me: I had written him off as a slacker based on that single impression. That was the meaning I had assigned him. I had not stopped to consider that there might be greatness in him.

The lesson to me was clear: Nothing is what you think it is. You give everything its meaning.

MY DAUGHTER HAS NO MEANING

In my class, I do an exercise in which I go around the room and ask participants to single out something in their lives—anything. Then I tell them to say that this thing has no meaning. I'm showing them that meaning isn't inherent in an object or person. So, for example, during my turn, I might say my job has no meaning, and the next person might say that his wife has no meaning. This might be followed by others saying the d. school has no meaning, their shoes have no meaning, their shirt has no meaning, their hair has no meaning, their weight has no meaning, their bike has no meaning, their math ability has no meaning. From minutiae to things that seem of obvious high importance, they're all lumped into the same category: things that have no intrinsic meaning.

After that the entire group starts mentioning items all at once so that no one is listening to one particular person and everyone is talking at the same time, each creating her own list of stuff that has no meaning in her life. It's a lot of noise and a lot of fun. The cacophony and pandemonium free people, so they don't feel as awkward saying out loud that things they otherwise hold dear have no meaning.

If you are alone you can still do this exercise. Saying things aloud, even to yourself, can be very freeing.

YOUR TURN

Take a few deep breaths. Close your eyes for a few minutes. Then open them and move your attention around the room from one object to another. Each time you notice an object, say it has no meaning (as in, "The chair has no meaning"). Then think of people in your family and in your life and things you hold dear, such as your biggest accomplishments and most prized possessions. Name each, saying it has no meaning. When you are finished, sit quietly for a few minutes and then reflect on your experience.

My colleague Sheri found it difficult to say that her daughter had no meaning. Of course her daughter has meaning, however, the meaning Sheri gives her daughter is not preordained. Some mothers abandon their daughters. Some mothers murder their daughters. Some disdain and deride them, and others cherish and support them. The variety of possible mother-daughter relationships and the meanings mothers attach to these relationships are endless.

The point of the exercise is not to get the participants to change any of their relationships. Rather, it is to empower them with the realization that they have *chosen* the meanings they give to all of their relationships. As a result, participants often become more aware of how important a person or item is to them (as in the case of Sheri, who cherished her relationship with her daughter even more after this exercise), and they realize that they have the ability to change the meaning something has to them.

For example, experiencing failure in an endeavor may initially be painful, but it is rarely catastrophic unless you give it that meaning. My colleague Georges was devastated when his son committed suicide after being jilted. The young lover took events that would probably be forgotten in short order and magnified them into literal life-and-death matters. It is easy to see the tragedy, both in the event itself and in the lack of perspective. Yet many of us lack this perspective, usually on a smaller scale, and it's hard to step back and see this in ourselves.

Once you understand that you can *choose* what meaning and importance to place on something, you can also understand that it is you, not external circumstances, who determines the quality of your life.

THERE IS NO PERMANENT RECORD

As is likely true for most people, there have been many incidents in my life about which I can now laugh, even though they seemed terrible at the time. The earliest I can remember was the day I came home for lunch in tears from my fourth-grade class. I had been making noise in the stairwell and a teacher, hearing me, told me that the offense would go on my "permanent record card." I was devastated, believing that this record would follow me forever. My mother attempted to soothe me, telling me it was nothing to be concerned about, but I couldn't be convinced. Of course, years later I figured out that there was no such thing as a permanent record card. And the bigger question is, even if there had been, would it have really made a difference in my life?

A similar incident happened in graduate school. I was much older and should have been much wiser—alas, I wasn't. I was studying for my PhD and took an advanced course, "Mathematical Methods in Physics," from a young Nobel Prize winner. The final examination relied heavily on some things well known to physics majors that I had not heard of and that had never been mentioned in the class. I got an F. When I talked to the professor about it, he told me, "Well, you are an engineer. If I took a music course, I would expect to fail too."

I didn't cry to my mother, otherwise the situation played out almost exactly as my fourth-grade trauma had. I was miserable and went to see my thesis professor. He assured me that it was nothing to be concerned about. Still, it bothered me for a long time. Eventually, of course, I discovered that no one cared about the F grade on my transcript. Even if they did, would it really have made a meaningful difference in my life? Nope. I did take the next course in the sequence, with another professor, and earned an A+. And guess what? No one noticed that either.

In life, typically, the only one keeping a scorecard of your successes and failures is you, and there are ample opportunities to learn the lessons you need to learn, even if you didn't get it right the first—or fifth—time.

LEARNING FROM BETRAYAL

During a workshop I ran in Bulgaria during the Cold War, I showed a videotape of some student robotics projects to the group. We broke for lunch, and when I asked for my tape back, I was told it had been locked away for safekeeping and that they were tracking down the person who had mistakenly left with the key.

The story seemed a little odd to me. Later in the afternoon I mentioned this to one of my friends who was also in the workshop. He told me in confidence that the delay was because a professor and his assistants—people I knew as friends—had taken my tape elsewhere to have it copied. Eventually my tape was returned, and they stuck with their original story about the reason for the delay. What nerve! I was hurt and angry that they had betrayed me and violated our friendship.

When I gave my second talk at the workshop, I spoke about scientific interchanges fostering friendship and trust. While doing this, I looked pointedly at the perpetrators. I was sure they understood that I knew what they had done and was slyly reprimanding them—still I wasn't satisfied. Upset, I went off into the woods to sulk by myself, thinking I would show them how wrong they were. I would leave early, skipping the gala closing banquet.

As I walked in the woods, I kept festering. Eventually, my "nothing has any meaning" exercise came to mind. I ran through the events of the day in my head, listing off each item and repeating that it had no meaning. When I got to "This tape has no meaning," a light bulb came on in my head. It could not have been truer. There was absolutely nothing on that tape of any special value to me or to them. What were they planning to do with it? I still don't know. Give it to their intelligence agency?

Show it to their students? Watch to get ideas for projects? I had already shown the tape; there was nothing private or ground-breaking on it. If they had asked, I would gladly have let them copy it, so what was the big deal? I had given the tape a meaning it did not really possess.

They should have asked, and they didn't. Big deal. Why was I about to let this ruin my night? Once I cleared my head, I returned to the hotel and ended up having a wonderful time at the banquet that evening.

This incident was a vivid reminder that while I cannot control what the outside world does, I can determine my own experience. Once you accept that *you* give everything in your life its meaning, you feel like the master of your life, not a powerless victim of circumstance and chance.

MODIFIED RADICAL

When my friend Ann got breast cancer and underwent a mastectomy, she wrote "Modified Radical," a lengthy poem about her experience that was published in the *New England Journal of Medicine* and later incorporated into a booklet she titled *Modified Radical and Other Cancer Poems*. The American Cancer Society distributed the booklet as a patient education tool, and it became a source of comfort and inspiration for many people. Ann received letters from readers telling her how much her poem had helped them. One very moving letter came from a surgeon telling her that even though he had performed many mastectomies, and his wife had undergone one, he had not deeply grasped the psychological aspects of the experience until he read Ann's poems. That was when I first noticed that Ann has the knack of turning personal adversity into positive experiences for herself and those around her.

A few years later Julian, Ann's fifty-nine-year-old husband, was diagnosed with Alzheimer's disease. She was able to care for Julian at home for the first few years. Eventually, though, his condition became too much for her to handle, so she moved him to a residential care facility about forty miles away. She visited him regularly, and I joined her once a month.

We would pick Julian up at the facility and drive him to a nearby lakeside park. There we would hold hands and walk slowly along the lake singing old folk songs like "Oh My Darling, Clementine" and, in honor of Julian's Scottish origins, "The Bonnie Banks o' Loch Lomond." Finally we would buy him an ice cream or something else for his still well-functioning sweet tooth. It was always a great time, full of warm feelings and fun, even on the days when it wasn't clear whether Julian recognized me. On the drive back home I always felt glad to be alive. I left looking forward to my next visit.

Ann chronicled how she and Julian continued to celebrate life in two books—*Alzheimer's, a Love Story* and *A Curious Kind of Widow*—that describe how after the initial shock of fear, anger, and dread, she decided they would go down the road together in a spirit of love. Her books were used by the Alzheimer's Association to give hope and guidance to many families. They also led to invitations to lecture to lay caregivers and medical professionals at workshops and conferences.

While Julian was sick I also had another friend with advanced Alzheimer's. He too had loving and concerned caregivers, but they were consumed by a sense of fear, tragedy, and loss, and he was ordered about like a child and kept under tight control.

When I visited my friend, I always felt very uncomfortable for him, and was glad to leave. There was no joy in that place. The contrast with Julian could not have been greater. Interestingly, pre-Alzheimer's, Julian and my other friend had been similar in almost every way, and their disease progression was essentially identical. Clearly, what made the difference was Ann's attitude. For me it remains a strong reminder of how once we understand we give everything in our life its meaning, we can begin to control what happens to us and even convert our own adversity into a gift to ourselves and our loved ones.

THE MEANING OF ACHIEVEMENT

At the risk of sounding immodest, I've won a lot of awards. I have drawers filled with them. They're nice to receive and sometimes the dinners are fun. However, the next morning when I wake up and look at them—the glass paperweight, the certificate—they don't really mean anything.

So it is with many of the hallmarks of "achievement," as people usually use the word. Getting on the honor roll, graduating from college, getting a high-paying job, getting a higher-paying job, being salesman of the month, getting the corner office, getting a company car, getting interviewed by the media, winning awards: this is what most people think of when they think of achievement. To me all this misses the mark.

Each of those things can be a genuine achievement—something that means something to you for more than a day—or each could just be a badge of importance that you use to show people that you're *somebody*. Do those things make you happy in and of themselves?

I know mega-millionaires who are miserable. They spend their money getting the fat sucked out of their love handles and hiring bodyguards because they're paranoid (maybe rightfully so) that people are out to get them. They're always concerned with outdoing themselves and making the next million and the next—and for what? Conversely, I know artists who barely scrape by yet are happy and fulfilled. Neither is a sure path to happiness or enlightenment; you can surely be rich *and* happy, but one doesn't necessarily follow the other.

Achievement for achievement's sake, then, is pretty hollow. It's the endless pursuit of a carrot on a stick as you race around a track. For me, real achievement is traveling to a foreign country, learning some of the language, and finding my way around on my own. Real achievement is learning to be self-sufficient. Real achievement is making lifelong friends.

In my mind and for the purposes of this book, I define *achievement* as having a good life; getting the job of living done in a satisfying way that nurtures the life force within us and within those we associate with. It entails developing some self-mastery to handle the difficult aspects of our lives and relationships. It involves finding something to do with our lives that engages us and gives us positive feedback. If we're doing it right, life shouldn't be a debilitating struggle, even if at times it takes considerable effort.

THE FAMILIAR UNFAMILIAR

To forge a new attitude toward the events and relationships in your life, you must learn to look at them with a fresh perspective. It's a common practice during creativity seminars to give participants a bag full of materials and tools and then a problem to solve. The materials and tools are usually everyday items. Their nominal use is obvious to all. You are then to use those materials in whatever ways you want to solve the problem; however, there isn't usually an obvious connection between the items and your problem. For instance, maybe you have to figure out how to create a communication device using a box of Cheerios, a hammer, tape, cotton balls, a hairbrush, and a bag of marbles.

Most people have a cognitive bias called functional fixedness that causes them to see objects only in their normal context. The use of the materials and tools in their ordinary way will generally lead to no workable solutions or, at the very most, mundane ones. The really exciting solutions come from overcoming functional fixedness and using these everyday items in new ways. To see the possibilities it is helpful to take the viewpoint that *nothing is what you think it is*. You need to make the familiar unfamiliar.

So, for example, a box of Cheerios is no longer only a breakfast cereal. It can be broken down into cardboard and wax paper. It is a source of biomass or a source of small chips and grains. It also can be made into a sludgy mixture. Similarly, a hammer is a weight, a source of metal and wood, and it can act as a mandrel, a seesaw, or a pendulum. Tape can be used to hold things together, and it also can be made into its own structural element in any desired shape. There are a number of creative ways you might use these items to fulfill the assignment.

The same dynamic can be applied to ourselves. Just as things in the material world can be transformed from their common use into something different, so too can behavior and relationships. It's difficult at first to break through preconceived notions, however once you do it, you'll find it opens the world up to you. Stop labeling things in their usual way. Mike is not a failure because his class project failed. You are not a loser because you lost your job. Make the familiar into the unfamiliar, and the result can be amazing and delightful, as opposed to dull, nonfunctional, and ordinary.

My first experience with the power of changing a fixed

perception came after a long day running an intensive creativity workshop. I was on break, and I was completely brain-dead. I was sitting by myself, relaxing in front of a large fountain. Suddenly, through my fog of fatigue, the fountain transformed from streams of water to countless particles bouncing off each other. It was an amazing experience. It was as if I was simply too tired to focus on the label *fountain*. I was simply there, experiencing its component parts.

If you stop labeling the world, your job, and your life, you may find that an amazing trajectory is there for the taking. Several of my favorite students never graduated. They were bright and capable, yet rather than "play the game," they chose a different path. Their parents were probably not thrilled in the beginning. Yet, perhaps unsurprisingly, when I occasionally run into one of these dropouts, I almost always find that she has made good life choices that have made her happy, and often made the world better to boot.

You can remove labels entirely; you can also relabel to great effect. Recent studies reinforce the idea that relabeling can change behavior. Experimenters have found statistical evidence that, for instance, if you ask people to *be voters*, you get more voter turnout than if you simply ask people *to vote*.[1] Similarly, if you ask people *not to be cheaters* there is less cheating than if you just ask people *not to cheat*. The inference is that people are more concerned with reinforcing their self-image than with their actions; thus, to change behavior, you first change self-image.

We all have ideas in our minds of what and who we are. We may have an accurate self-image, or it may be way off. Either way, it strongly colors how we respond to the world around us. In her book *Mindset: The New Psychology of Success*, Carol Dweck writes, "For twenty years, my research has shown that *the view you adopt for yourself* profoundly affects the way you lead your life. It can determine whether you become the person you want to be and whether you accomplish the things you value."[2]

Occasionally we have powerful, life-changing experiences; but most changes take place in small increments. Some unexpected positive or negative experience will change your self-image slightly. Through repeated incremental changes, the entire image is altered. Done the right way, this increases your sense of what you can accomplish; psychologists say your self-efficacy is increased.

This happened to Doug when he decided he could control his late-onset diabetes blood sugar problem by riding his bike three times a week from his home on the Stanford campus to the mountain community of Sky Londa. The round trip is roughly twenty miles, with a change of elevation of about fifteen hundred feet. All went well in the beginning. Then he started to notice how much trash there was on the road. At first he thought only, Somebody should clean that up. Soon it dawned on him that "somebody" could be him. So he started to carry a plastic shopping bag with him, stopping periodically to pick up some cans and other trash. Slowly this grew into a new persona for him. He eventually was hauling large amounts of trash on his bicycle, single-handedly keeping a good portion of the road trash-free.

As Doug's activity became more known, he received increasing positive reinforcement from people living in the area. More and more drivers called out to him, some offering him money to reward his endeavor. He was guest of honor at a community party, stories were written in local newspapers, a movie was made about his road cleaning,[3] and he received environmental awards from San Mateo County. He became a local celebrity.

His self-image had altered considerably from the Doug who thought only, Somebody should clean that up. He was now "environmental Doug" or, as I lovingly dubbed him, Professor Poubelle ("dustbin," in French).

The concept of self-efficacy has been used to deal with phobias and other limiting states and, of course, in most psychotherapy.[4] Similar ideas have also been used in education and in creating pathways to successful living. In an ideal world, self-image would form the basis for much of what we do and do not do. In the real world, things are more complicated.

WHO CONTROLS YOUR BRAIN?

We generally like to think we are in charge of our actions. Society has a stake in us believing that, or there would be no way to justify restraining and punishing people with antisocial behaviors. Nevertheless, we know that some of the things we do are not controlled consciously. These are known as reflexive or autonomous behaviors.

It is easy to see these autonomous behaviors in other species. Some of these can be quite complex and are part of animals' DNA. For example, the South African weaverbird normally builds an intricate nest using specialized materials. Experimenters removed a pair of these birds from contact with building materials and from other members of their species for five generations.[5] The birds were not able to build, or even see, traditional nests. And yet when the sixth generation—still in isolation from its species—was given access to the traditional materials, it built a perfect nest. This may be an extreme example, yet it illustrates the point that even some complex behaviors may be reflexive and not quite under conscious control.

You see this at work when physical danger and emotional

threats trigger our fight-or-flight response. By the time the signals get to the parts of our brains that can reason about them, our emotional and reflexive brain centers have already armed our bodies, and we are in action.

Although this quick gut-level response could be lifesaving, it may not be the appropriate response to perceived emotional threats in a psychologically complex world. Not all issues can be satisfactorily resolved by following our first reactions. Like when that jerk cuts you off by swerving into your lane at ninety miles an hour.

What happens when someone does something aggressive on the highway? Well, most people respond in exactly the wrong way. They decide to *fight*. They yell, curse, honk their horns, or even chase and attempt to confront the offending driver. Meanwhile, the best option for survival is *flight*. I have discussed this with people from many different backgrounds, and it always brings the same response. We all agree that if someone is driving aggressively or dangerously, the best thing to do is stay as far away as possible. Yet a lot of us admit to behaving in the opposite manner: we pursue the other car. Where does that come from? In this situation there are two options. The first is the initial knee-jerk reaction triggered by our brain, which is out of our conscious control. The second is our reasoned response, which can be brought under control.

The first reaction is often called a *limbic-abduction reaction* or an *amygdala hijacking* because it is triggered by the amygdala, a small organ within the brain's limbic system. The amygdala's primary function is to immediately signal the adrenal glands when a fear stimulus is received. It has a secondary—and slower—connection to the cortex and the other reasoning centers of the brain.

It is important to realize that the secondary "reasoned" re-action is not a voluntary one. Many of us just follow what we have seen our friends and family do, and that can brainwash us into thinking that dysfunctional behavior is the normal or honorable thing. With a bit of effort you can easily change your secondary reaction. All you have to do is decide you want to change, and then work on it. If you are willing to ignore the initial limbic impulse, you can get your cortex to calm down, take charge, and calm your whole body down.

Admittedly, some people have to work harder at controlling themselves than others. It does not matter if you're a hothead by nature or nurture (or both), you can learn to control your secondary reaction, and it's important to do this, so you don't end up blowing up at people. Some powerful people—politicians, actors, singers, CEOs, even a book publisher—have ruined their careers because they didn't get their limbic impulses under control. Momentary temper flare-ups can cost you everything.

Harvard University neurology professor Rudy Tanzi recommends a four-step process to handle situations in which we are in the thrall of a *limbic abduction*:

- Stop yourself from doing what your initial reaction dictated.
- Take a deep breath.
- Become aware of how you are feeling.
- Recall a past event that gave you a feeling of happiness and peace.[6]

In terms of design thinking, you're breaking down the fight response and looking at it as a problem to be solved, then using ideation to bring you to a better place. These steps bring you into a state of emotional well-being, in which you regain control over your behavior.

In most cases you only need to take the first three steps to get the situation under control. It takes practice (i.e., in terms of design thinking, making prototypes), and if you keep at it every time a negative behavior presents itself, it eventually becomes easier and easier to gain control and stop doing it. In any event, taking a deep breath in any situation never hurts.

USE YOUR BRAIN

What about other, less immediate situations? Can these techniques help us respond more positively to a more general stressful state? The answer is yes. If you take time to be aware of your current mental state and then deliberately alter it, you can force your brain into more balanced activities. Eventually, this de-stressing becomes automatic.

Various types of dysfunctional behavior are associated with a lack of balance in the use of different parts of our brains. So, for example, pathological eating is associated with the reptilian part of your brain (the brain stem). Narcissistic or overly dramatic behavior is associated with being stuck in the emotional (limbic) part of the brain. Overintellectualization is associated with being stuck in the part associated with higher intellectual functions (the neocortex).

We can stop ourselves from getting stuck by practicing self-awareness. In this way we can train our brains to give us greater sensory awareness, body awareness, and social awareness. This is generally referred to as mind over matter, the main principle behind cognitive behavioral therapy, a school of psychology that believes if we can change our thinking, we can change our behavior. Though it doesn't always work for everyone, it's a method I encourage. No matter what got you to the state you're in, consciously changing the way you think about it can help solve the problem.

YOUR TURN

Who am I? What do I want? What is my purpose? Ask yourself each of these questions repeatedly and respond with whatever comes to mind. You can write out your answers in a journal or notebook, or just say them to yourself. Don't overthink; just answer the questions. It's okay to repeat yourself, and it's okay to say things that don't make a lot of sense. Each question should be repeated for at least five or ten minutes. If you have someone available to work with, you can take turns where one person repeatedly asks the same question and the other person answers. Of course, if there are two people, the questions need to be rephrased: "Who are you?" "What do you want?" "What is your purpose?" (I might answer: I am a father, I am a husband; I want to finish my book, I want more time; my purpose is to teach, my purpose is to live. All of these are, for me, on a superficial level. Usually it takes a little while to come up with insightful rather than mundane answers. Do it! You might be surprised with what you come up with, and how it contributes to your achievement habit.)

The effect of this exercise is to get you to devote time to thinking deeply about the meaning of your life. What matters more than your specific answers is that you open yourself to these questions. Doing this exercise generally promotes relaxation, builds internal energy, and nurtures an increased sense of aliveness.

Similar benefits can be derived from other types of meditation. Experiment to see which works best for you. I rarely meditate in a formal manner; instead I do things that are meditative. I take walks. I ride my bike. I make time to be alone in nature when I need to quiet my mind. Another thing that works for some people is repetitive activities that require little focus. Knitting, crocheting, gardening, and doodling can all be meditative. Or make it even simpler! If you're feeling scattered, you can just take a few minutes to be still and focus on your breathing. Be mindful of each breath: in and out, in and out. Try to make your exhalation last twice as long as your inhalation. Pay attention to a fixed object around you—books, a picture on the wall; don't analyze, just ground yourself. Ultimately you will benefit from increased concentration, decreased anxiety, and a general feeling of happiness.

RIGHT AND WRONG

In life we will often find ourselves playing the game of right and wrong. The rules *seem* quite simple: I win if I am right—and you are wrong.

I once had a heated disagreement with my wife, Ruth, about something silly just as I was leaving to walk over to my friend Doug's house. As I was walking, I was consumed with thoughts of how right I was and how wrong she was. She was worse than wrong. She was downright pigheaded and stupid about it. I was consumed by such thoughts for about two blocks. And then I looked up.

It was a beautiful clear winter day, and the bare trees had a fantastic presence. I was awestruck. I felt a surge of wonderment and joy. Still consumed by my feelings about the argument, I shook my head and descended back into my self-righteous annoyance. I put my head down and kept walking and thinking about how stupid she was being. Then I looked up again, allowed myself to experience the wonderment, and again shut it down. I couldn't seem to let my feelings go.

Finally enlightenment came. By continuing to play my solitaire hand of right and wrong, I was being downright pigheaded and stupid. The world was offering me a magic moment, and I was turning it down. With that realization I was able to laugh at my stupidity and enjoy the moment. I arrived at Doug's house in a euphoric state. That incident took place over twenty years ago. I have no memory of what the argument was about, and each winter I again feel the wonder of that experience when I look up at the bare trees.

This whole situation is kind of like gambling in a card room. The room gets its percent off the top the minute you start to play each hand—it's how it makes its money. Clearly, regardless of whether you win or lose specific hands, at the end of the night the players' total worth will have been diminished—it is the price of playing. If I had continued playing the right and wrong game that day, I would have lost a peak experience, and the card room would have gotten much more from me than its usual fee.

Whenever I find myself challenged to a game of right and wrong, I stop playing. Next time you find yourself playing right and wrong, remember: You give everything in your life its meaning, so you can choose to end the game. It does not matter how right you are or how wrong they are; you lose just by playing.

SIMILARLY, YOU CAN MODIFY the way you react to experiences. One little trick is that by exaggerating your reaction, you can make the experience better. For example, if you are at a boring meeting, just tell yourself that it is the most boring meeting you have ever attended. It is in fact *so boring* that it is amazing. If you are depressed, do not get depressed at the idea of being depressed. Get off on it. Admire the fact that you are having this amazing depression.

It's the opposite of wallowing; it's allowing yourself to become amused by the terribleness of your situation. You know how some dogs are so ugly they're cute? This is like that. Think of the metaphors a comedian would use to describe just how bad the meeting is. Write your troubles into a comedic country song. Deliver your own stand-up routine about depression.

It's incredibly empowering to realize that you have the power to change your attitude toward anything. Do you hate washing dishes? If you think about it, there is a lot that is nice about washing dishes. Putting your hands into warm water is soothing. Rinsing and soaping can be a pleasure. And getting rid of a mess and admiring your clean kitchen is always satisfying. Try out a new attitude toward dish washing. You might just find enjoyment in it.

ONCE YOU LEARN THAT it is possible to change your habits and develop new attitudes about things, you have a new tool to use in both your professional and your personal life. For most people it is probably easier to change their attitude toward dishwashing than their attitude toward depression. Yet if you start with the small stuff, you will find it easier to tackle the harder stuff in life.

REASONS
ARE
bullshit

CHAPTER 2

Obviously the truth is what's so.
Not so obviously, it is also so what.
—*Werner Erhard*

The problem with reasons is that they're just excuses prettied up.

I always used to be late to the board meeting of Working Machines, a corporation located in Berkeley, an hour from where I live. Invariably, after a frantic hour of aggressive and dangerous driving, I would arrive with an apology, explaining that the highway was unusually congested. The board chairman always graciously assured me that the main thing was that I had arrived safely. Still, I had held things up, and the other board members, who had arrived on time, were clearly not thrilled. Deep down I knew that the highway traffic was not the real issue.

Yes, the traffic on highway 880 was often heavier than I had hoped it would be, and the traffic getting out of Palo Alto and into Berkeley was excruciatingly slow. Yet how unusual was heavy midday traffic, really? I merely failed to allow enough time. I *tried* to leave earlier. Yet I would always squeeze in a few last-minute e-mails and phone calls. Then, after leaving my office, I would see a colleague at the elevator and get caught up in a discussion.

It all came down to this: I did not see the meeting as a high priority in my life. It was that simple. It had nothing to do with the traffic. Although there were no negative business consequences, it was bad for my self-esteem: I felt guilty for always being late. I didn't like how it felt to have all eyes on me for the wrong reason when I walked into the room. I gave it some thought and realized that there were other people in that room facing the same traffic and the same "life happens" stuff that I was, yet they managed to be there before me because they cared enough to do so.

Once I had that insight, I decided that from then on I would give the meeting the priority it deserved. Thereafter, I gave the meeting the *attention* it required and left early enough to get there on time. No more last-minute e-mails or phone calls, no cutting it close. I stopped waiting until the last minute, and decided that it was worth it to stop everything else early and get in the car ten minutes before I "had to."

If I was lucky, and the traffic was very light, I had time to enjoy a little of the Berkeley scene before I went into the meeting. If traffic was normal, I was a little early and could schmooze with some of the other board members. If traffic was really ugly, I was just on time. The positive effects of eliminating the stress associated with getting to the meetings on time were life-changing.

And it didn't end there. I began to change my attitude toward time overall. I used to be late to most things in my life. Now I am known as the pain in the ass who is always on time and expects others to be. I make it a point to start every class and every workshop session on time. It turns out that my life works better when I do not need to come up with reasons for why I am late.

Our society loves reasons. Perhaps the illusion that there is a single known reason for each thing we do is comforting. Unfortunately, the world doesn't work that way. There's the story of the man who is standing in the middle of Times Square in Manhattan, snapping his fingers. A woman comes up to him after some time and says, "Pardon me, sir, why are you snapping your fingers?"

He replies, "I am keeping the tigers away."

She says, "Sir, except for the zoo, there's not a tiger for thousands of miles."

"Pretty effective, isn't it?" he says.

This joke uses what is called a causal fallacy. The fallacy comes because the finger snapper mistakenly believes that *correlation implies causation*. This is just one of several logical fallacies in which two events that occur at the same time are taken to have a cause-and-effect relationship. This version of the fallacy is also known as *cum hoc ergo propter hoc* (Latin for "with this, therefore because of this") or, simply, false cause. A similar fallacy—that an event that follows another was a consequence of the first—is described as *post hoc ergo propter hoc* (Latin for "after this, therefore because of this").

Reasons are bullshit. I know it sounds harsh, however, it's a good categorical stand to take, as you'll see. Reasons exist because if people didn't explain their behavior, they would seem unreasonable. So we are faced with a paradox: we need reasons so we appear reasonable, yet when we use reasons we are not taking full responsibility for our behavior.

Let's say I walk up to a stranger and punch him in the face. He'll ask why I did that. If I say, "For no reason," I am clearly unreasonable. If instead I say he reminds me of the man who abused my sister, I am now a (somewhat) reasonable person.

Reasons are often just excuses, however. We use them to hide our shortcomings from ourselves. When we stop using reasons to justify ourselves, we increase our chances of changing behavior, gaining a realistic self-image, and living a more satisfying and productive life.

Many reasons are simply excuses to hide the fact that we are not willing to give something a high enough priority in our lives. For example, a student might come into my class late, saying, "I'm sorry I'm late. I got a flat on my bicycle." Even if it is true that her bicycle has a flat tire, the bottom line is, getting to class on time is not a high enough priority in her life. If I had a rule that any student who came in late would fail the class, she would have made sure to be on time, flat tire or not. If the rule was you got expelled from school for a single lateness, she would have been there even earlier!

A *GOOOOOD* REASON

In the Design Group at Stanford University, most colleagues have participated in my workshops, and they all know how I feel about "reasons." So anyone who starts to give reasons at a meeting—say, for example, "I could not do that because the dean . . ."—is often treated to a sarcastic chorus of "That's a *goooood* reason," after which he gets a bit embarrassed. However, he has received, as a gift, the insight that the dean is not the reason.

Letting go of the need for reasons to justify your behavior is useful in every part of the design thinking process. It can get you unstuck from dead ends, and lead to new approaches and insights.

YOUR TURN

This exercise ideally involves a partner, though you can do it alone, playing both roles. One partner gives a statement, starting with "The reason I . . ." The other partner responds, "That's a *goooood* reason." Do this for about five minutes, then reverse the roles so that the second partner starts the conversation with "The reason I . . . ," and the first partner now affirms each such statement as being a *goooood* reason. (To get the most out of this exercise, use your current behaviors. For example, this morning I might say, "The reason I am writing this book is that I want to share my knowledge." My partner would respond, "That's a *goooood* reason." Then I would say, "The reason I am tired is that I got up too early." My partner would respond, "That's a *goooood* reason." And so on.)

You won't have to search within your answers very long to find the bullshit. If you find that you resist the idea that all your reasons are *goooood* reasons, it will be useful for you to think of several additional reasons for each behavior. Many factors contribute to a given behavior, so the entire concept of emphasizing one particular reason for something becomes muddled. In assigning relative importance to our reasons, we introduce a lie into our analysis—we add a high weighting factor to the reasons that most support our version of the story or our self-image.

Sometimes people hide behind heart-wrenching reasons. It is important to understand that this doesn't make them any more useful.

Steve, my oldest son, was born with cerebral palsy, which in his case meant both mental retardation and muscular spasticity. Although he has a tough time doing things that others find easy, he can manage most everyday things. When his mother reprimands him for bad manners, such as not using a knife to cut his food, he gets angry and says, "I can't help it. I was born that way." Whenever he says that, my heart goes out to him. Still, it is in his best interest to realize that he is giving us a *goooood* reason.

REASONS AND THEIR COMPLICATIONS

Studies have shown that people are selective when it comes to recording what really happens to and around them. No matter how strongly you feel you have the true picture, you are probably wrong. You can't know the reason for anyone's behavior.

To complicate matters further, sometimes we are actively dishonest about the reasons for our behavior.[1] A classic example comes from a Japanese professor in one of my workshops. He claimed he wanted to spend more time with his family, but he was too busy at work. When I asked a few questions and elicited some details about his daily activity, it was clear that he wasted a lot of time at work. He chose to stay late at the university, socialize with his colleagues during the evenings, and then appear macho by having it known that he went home later than everyone else while receiving sympathy for not being able to spend more time with his family. Clearly he had made a choice, and being too busy at work was, of course, bullshit as a reason. This was immediately obvious to everyone in the workshop, yet it took me a full half hour to get a glimmer of recognition out of him.

Things happen; we do things, and others do things. If you like what happens, keep doing what you are doing and hope it keeps working well. If you do not like what happens, do it differently next time. Reasons get in the way of this simple pragmatic approach.

We are far better off without reasons. They provide people

with excuses to keep behaving dysfunctionally. The world would be a much better place without reasons, right?

Okay, yes, not having reasons would lead to a strange existence. Without reasons, you would look like an unreasonable person to everyone else. So where does this leave us?

I have a twofold approach to the problem: one for the external persona, and one for the internal self. *Externally* you use reasons in everyday conversation when you need to, and thus appear to be perfectly normal and reasonable. *Internally* you look at the reasons your external self offers, and question each of them. The internal self also looks at the reasons given by the people you are interacting with. Simply by noticing how reasons are used, you can gain insight into your own behavior and your relationships with others.

This approach works well to change your own actions. It can't be used to change others, however! It is not your job to tell anyone else her reasons are bullshit unless she is actively seeking your advice (like taking your class or, say, reading your book); doing this would make you a pretty unlikable person pretty quickly. The best way to fix the world is to fix yourself. As I always caution my students and workshop participants, do not try this (on anyone else) at home!

Make a pact with yourself to not use reasons unless you have to. This is actually an incredibly empowering position to come from. Be confident enough in your actions not to need to explain yourself. Trust yourself and act.

I get a lot of requests from students around the world who want to join my research group at Stanford. If I know I will not accept them, I simply thank them for their interest and say I am sorry that I will not be able to accommodate them. This invariably ends the conversation. I get at most a thank-you note.

However, if I justify my action with a reason, then the conversation drags on as the student attempts to work around my reason. In the past I have given a bullshit reason; it feels like I'm being nicer somehow. Sure, it may be true that I'm too busy or going on sabbatical soon, or whatever else I've told the student, yet if I felt strongly enough about that person, I'd make it happen. In truth, it is difficult to think of a *goooood* reason I could not work around if I really wanted to.

Actions speak louder than reasons. Don't give reasons unless you have to!

SAYING THE OPPOSITE

Often we say the opposite of what we really mean when faced with beliefs or behavior we find troubling. I recall a very aggressive young colleague of mine who had developed a grievance against a prestigious and long-standing robotics conference. He launched a new conference meant to be in direct competition with the original one. When I asked what his motivation was, he said, "The last thing I would want to do is undermine the existing conference, but there is a need for a new conference."

It had not occurred to me that his motivation was to undermine the existing conference until he said that. Once he denied the unmade accusation, it was clear that undermining was indeed what he intended. He had projected his own guilt onto me in the form of an accusation that I had never made.

Have you heard the expression "He doth protest too much"? Often, if someone goes to great lengths to tell you that he is not a liar, a crook, a troublemaker, or green with envy, he probably *is* those things.

I am sure we all have at one time or another said the opposite of what we mean—and let's face it, as much as we like to convince ourselves that our motives are pure, we are generally most concerned about ourselves. To keep this in check, do a reversal in your head. Anytime you or someone else gives a motive for behavior, just substitute in your head the opposite of that motive. So, for example, if you say, "I am telling Kathy what her coworker said about her for *her* benefit, not mine," try out the reverse motivation in your head: "I am telling her for *my* benefit, not hers." Often you will find that this is your true motive.

PROJECTION

Projection is a common response. It happens when someone attributes a feeling or trait to another person, when it's she herself who owns that particular trait or feeling. Although psychologists usually use the term *projection* to connote a negative behavior, projecting both the positive and the negative aspects of ourselves onto others is an important part of life that can be a major influence on our interactions with others. It is the experience of seeing traits in others that helps us to see them in ourselves. If you notice a flaw in another person, it probably means you've had that same flaw yourself.

Projection colors almost every aspect of interpersonal relations. A genuinely naive, truthful person will think all people he encounters are truthful. A person with a background of duplicity and dishonesty tends to be wary of others because he projects his own manipulative behavior onto them. Once we project a behavior onto others, it gives us a *goooood* reason to think we know what accounts for their behavior.

As you now know, I cannot stand to be late because lateness is an issue in my life. So I assume that others share the same concern. When people are late, I cannot understand how they could be so irresponsible. However, only after I became obsessed with being on time did I even notice lateness in others.

YOUR TURN

One way to see how prevalent projections are is to make a list of things that bother you about other people in your life. Then take these same things and think about how they appear in your own life. For example, I'd say, "I hate how my son Elliot bickers with his friend Claudia" since, not surprisingly, "I hate how I bicker with my wife."

There are countless things to like or dislike about people. That I chose to mention bickering first says something about me. It tells me that bickering is such an important issue to me that I project my feelings about it onto my son. Realizing this provides a great tool for self-awareness, and such insights make us more empathetic about others' difficulties.

Self-hatred plays a large part in this aspect of our personalities. In chapter 4 of *The Adjusted American*, the book I mentioned earlier, Snell and Gail Putney explore this concept: "Men hate in others those things and only those things which they despise in themselves. It is possible to disapprove of other people in a rational and dispassionate manner, however, to hate them is an irrational and impassioned act. The passion betrays the underlying self-contempt. . . . The origin of hatred lies in the individual's attempt to disown certain potentialities of the self."

In other words, if we sense, even subconsciously, traits within ourselves that we would rather not acknowledge because they are alien to our self-image, we deny their existence and project them onto others. Thus our hatred of others is really the hatred of our own unwanted or feared capabilities projected onto them. To get beyond the self-destructive effects of hatred, it is necessary to be able to accept a basic truth about ourselves: *we are all potentially capable of any human act.*

LOVE AND MARRIAGE

Projection also plays a large role in Putney and Putney's provocative assertion that *marriage for love is a bad idea* (chapter 10). Put in our terms, they are saying that getting married for love is a *goooood* reason. For many of my students, this is a version of the aforementioned yellow-eyed cat story. They have all been brought up with the notion that marrying for love is not only desirable, it is also one of life's highest possible attainments.

A friend once told me he was in love with falling in love. I knew what he meant. It can be a great feeling to fall in love—especially if your love is reciprocated. Incidentally, when he did eventually marry for love, it turned out to be a disaster. The problem is that people often confuse love with marriage. Falling in love is heavily reliant on projection, while a sound marriage is relatively free of projection.

Just as hatred is the result of projecting our own negative qualities onto another, love is the result of projecting our own positive qualities onto another. What we fall in love with are the qualities that we wish we had or qualities we have and wish to share with the other person. Usually these admired qualities are at variance with our self-image, so we avoid consciously possessing them ourselves and instead project them onto another. In time these idealized projections are worn away by life's realities. Any marriage based mainly on projected qualities is bound to flounder.

A successful marriage results when both partners can just be happy being who they are and in so doing add to the enjoyment of each other. As the Putneys point out, "Each is seeking candor and warmth, and the exploration of self-potential (sexual capacities and many others), all of which is facilitated by cooperation of someone else engaged in a similar development. Such persons are not preoccupied with being loved or with maintaining romantic illusions. They are trying to enjoy life—together."

Love is the ultimate unreasonable activity. When asked why you love your significant other, you might say, "She's smart and has a great smile and is kind to animals," but clearly those reasons are only half true. You could find lots of women who are just as smart and who have great smiles and also love animals. Why don't you love *all* of them? No one knows exactly why he falls in love. The Putneys call it projection; you can call it chemistry or fate or whatever you want; you're drawn to whom you're drawn to and attracted to whom you're attracted to, and whatever reasons you give yourself are probably bullshit.

I used to look down on the institution of arranged marriage; surprisingly my attitude changed completely when I visited India and spent time in the homes of the people there. I saw just as much or more genuine affection between husbands and wives there than I did in America. I now feel that young Indians are quite lucky to have a culture where people who love them and know them well set about to assist them in finding suitable marriage partners.

The idea that marriage is a joining of entire families, not just two isolated people, is also very attractive. It is not a perfect system: there can be compulsion and ulterior motives on the part of the parents. In my experience, however, that is rare among educated families. If both parties are given veto power, then I believe the system is in many ways superior to online dating and the bar scenes that seem to be the major options these days for single people in America. The basic difference is that in America, a man marries the woman he loves; in India, a man loves the woman he marries.

DECISION AND INDECISION

When you make a decision about something, you always need a *goooood* reason. It's easy to agonize over even the smallest decisions. My wife and son are incredibly indecisive. My son always waits until the last minute. His mind-set is, Why commit before you absolutely have to? A better opportunity may come along. It may work for him, however, it is tough on the people around him. My wife sees the negatives in every option, so is reluctant to choose something that is not perfect.

My wife and son are victims of the Buridan's ass paradox, named after the fourteenth-century French philosopher Jean Buridan and based on an old fable about a donkey that dies because it cannot make a rational choice between two equally appealing alternatives—eat hay or drink water. This fable has given rise to the Buridan's ass method, in which the decision is based on eliminating the option that has the most negatives so that you don't end up like the donkey. My wife has essentially reinvented this method, whereas my son is often in danger of starving to death by virtue of indecision.

I still chuckle over the time I was in France and came to a T intersection. The sign pointing to the left and the sign pointing to the right both had the name of the same village. I pulled over and spent many minutes, brow furrowed, wondering whether to go right or left. Of course, in the end it didn't matter which way I went; both roads led to the same place! We would all do well to remember the old saying "If you don't know where you are going, it doesn't matter which road you choose."

Making important decisions only after due consideration is a good way to live one's life. However, people often let the agony of deciding go on far too long. Like the fabled donkey, they have all the relevant information, yet they can't decide.

In advising my students on making a big life decision, I find that after they've laid out the problem in question and we have discussed the pros and cons of each option, it's best to introduce what I call the gun test. It's very scientific, you see. I point my fingers, in the form of a gun, at the student's forehead and say, "Okay, you have fifteen seconds to decide or I'll pull the trigger. What's your decision?"

They always know the answer! Even if they do not ultimately take that path, this exercise usually releases the pressure built up around the decision-making process and gets them closer to a resolution.

I've named another tool I use the life's journey method. If a student presents a problem with two possible paths to a solution, I ask the student to take one of the choices and then imagine what life would look like as a result of that choice. It might go something like this:

STUDENT: Okay, I decide to go for the PhD.

ME: Then what happens?

STUDENT: I get the PhD.

ME: Great; then what happens?

STUDENT: I graduate and get a job as a professor.

ME: Great; then what happens?

STUDENT: I get married and buy a house.

ME: Great; then what happens?

STUDENT: I have children.

ME: Great; then what happens?

STUDENT: My children grow up and get married.

ME: Great; then what happens?
STUDENT: I get older.
ME: Great; then what happens?
STUDENT: I die.

Then I ask the student to imagine her life if she took the other path. It might go like this:

STUDENT: I would leave school after my master's degree.
ME: Then what happens?
STUDENT: I get a job in industry, or I start a company.
ME: Great; then what happens?
STUDENT: I make a lot of money.
ME: Great; then what happens?
STUDENT: I do the marriage, kids, house thing.
ME: Great; then what happens?
STUDENT: I get old and die.
ME: So the end is the same. No matter what path you take, in the end you die.

The point of this is to get people to realize that there is no way to know where a decision will lead. The best way forward is embedded in the design thinking methodology: manifest a bias toward action, and don't be afraid of failure. I believe it serves people best in life to accept that decisions are part of the process of moving forward, and that there are so many variables that it's a waste of time to try to see the endgame. Once we realize that most decisions are not life-or-death, we can make them without undue stress.

Now, much of this flies in the face of decision analysis theory, which presents analytical methods to make good decisions even in the face of imprecise information. Unfortunately, for decisions on personal matters quantitative tools can be inadequate to capture the subtleties, and thus yield misleading conclusions.

Many years ago I was living in India, in the guest house of the Indian Institute of Science in Bangalore. Kumar, a young engineer who visited me every few days, told me that he was leaving and would be gone for three weeks. He'd be taking the train to his native village in the north to choose a bride. His family had located six eligible candidates, and he was going to meet with them, decide who was the most suitable, and marry her.

A month later Kumar reappeared, carrying a rolled-up window shade. When he unrolled it, I saw that he had crafted a large and complex weighted decision table, a standard tool used in decision analysis theory. On it were listed the names of the six prospective brides, each row representing one of the women. Each of seven columns was headed by an attribute he was most interested in. Each woman had been numerically rated for each attribute, from 1 to 10, and each of these numbers was multiplied by the weighting factor he'd given that attribute, according to what he deemed its relative importance. The seven weighting factors were chosen so that they added up to 10. If he had rated the attributes equally, all the weighting factors would have been 10/7 (which we can round off to be approximately 1.4).

Names	Appearance	Personality	Attraction	Education	Career	Wealth	Family	Total
Name 1	8	10	14.4	15	7.2	5	12	71.6
Name 2	7.2	16	18	12	5.4	8	18	84.6
Name 3	7.2	14	10.8	10.5	4.5	6	16	69.1
Name 4	6.4	18	12.6	6	1.8	6	14	64.8
Name 5	8	8	12.6	10.5	3.6	4	12	58.7
Name 6	6.4	12	16.2	13.5	7.2	8	18	81.3

The column at the end showed the sum of the seven numbers in that row. The woman corresponding to the column with the highest total—the second woman in the table—would be the chosen bride. Very rational—just what I would have expected from a good engineer. However, the more he told me about his meetings with the women, the clearer it became that this was not as rational as he pretended.

There were two major departures from objectivity: first, of course, was the fact that the scores that he gave each woman were totally subjective. Second was that he was not completely honest with himself about his weighting factors. For example, he told me he gave "wealth" a low weighting factor of 1 because he did not care about his wife's wealth. Yet he weighted "family" twice as high. When I asked what he looked for when he rated the family, his answer told me that he was looking for things that indicated that the family was wealthy.

The most confused of all seemed to be the ratings for "career." Kumar told me he definitely wanted his wife to have a career and not stay at home, and he also wanted her to be available to take care of dinner if, at the last minute, he decided to invite some of his work colleagues to his house. So he gave this a low weighting of 0.9.

When all was said, it was clear that he had fudged the numbers in favor of the women he felt most connected to during their short meeting. So much for analytical thinking! (As it turned out, intuition worked just fine: Kumar and his wife have been happily married for over twenty-five years.)

Decision making has become a big business, and new tools are being developed all the time. All of them, however, rest on a belief and a value system that require logical systematic thought.

This approach appeals to people who are naturally judgmental and value so-called rational thought. If it could deliver good decisions at most of life's crossroads, it would be terrific. Unfortunately, it often can't.

In my experience, quantitative methods and feelings both have their places. I tend to be pragmatic, and I don't discount my intuition. If a tool gives me good answers, I use it. In either case, when making decisions, it couldn't hurt to keep in mind Captain Ahab's realization about his pursuit of Moby Dick: "All my means are sane, *my motive and my object mad.*"

The best scientific methods for decision making won't help if your question is one that can't be answered rationally. Ahab was following a logical course of action, but he was doing that in pursuit of something irrational. Make sure that your motive is a good one before bothering to figure out how you'll find an answer.

DON'T LISTEN TO YOUR PROFESSOR

I had a PhD student from Bulgaria whose father was a well-known professor, and the student had led a fairly privileged life in his country. He was very bright and inquisitive.

After a while he started asking me questions about things in this country that confused him. For example, in Bulgaria there was one nationwide price for gasoline. He could not understand how some gas stations in the United States could charge more than the others and survive. He asked, "Wouldn't everyone go to the least expensive station?"

At the time I didn't really know the answer to that question. Of course, now that I have the d.school mentality, I would probably tell him to go ask the people buying gas at the expensive stations! Regardless, it was fascinating to see America through his questioning eyes.

Then one day he came to me with a serious problem. He had begun to realize that it was impossible to do lots of things without a credit card. He couldn't rent videos or a car, and many places would ask for a second form of identification, which he didn't have. The problem was that he couldn't get a card unless he already had credit. I decided to let him apply for a joint card with me.

The deal was this: I would not use the card, and paying the bill would be his sole responsibility. We received two cards in the mail, and I destroyed mine. A few days later he came to me with a mailing he had received. As a bonus for applying for the card, we were eligible to buy a packet of tickets for the Canadian lottery in British Columbia. For only twenty dollars we had the chance to win valuable prizes. He asked me what I thought. I gave him my best New York streetwise explanation of what a sucker play it was. I told him to throw the offer in the garbage. Furthermore, even if it was an honest offer, he was certainly smart enough to figure how ridiculously poor the odds of his winning were. Certainly these were *goooood* reasons not to do it.

Close your eyes and imagine the end of this story.

Got it? Okay.

Here is what actually happened. He sent in his twenty dollars, and he won the grand prize: a luxury car or $80,000 Canadian. He took the money, which came tax-free because he was an alien. He and his fiancée used the money for their wedding and for a down payment on a house. They soon had children, and they are now living happily ever after in California.

This was yet another time I'm glad someone did not listen to my rational voice of experience and expertise. I guess when it comes to the accidents of real life, not even professors know much. The point of the story isn't to ignore all advice. It's that you have to live with the consequences, good or bad. Do something or don't do it. Follow advice or ignore it. In making your decisions, keep in mind that even when the odds are against you, you still might win. Life is a gamble, and ultimately you have to decide for yourself.

WHO'S REALLY STOPPING YOU?

If there's something you really want to do, often it's as simple as just doing it. Remember, I am talking about the real stuff, not pipe dreams. In the end you don't need tricks or gimmicks. It comes down to the difference between *trying* and *doing*, between *talking about it* and *acting*; and ultimately it depends on the double bottom line: *intention* and *attention*. Do you really intend to do it? Are you willing to give it the attention it requires?

If so, then you simply need to start. In design thinking parlance, it's time to enact what we call the *bias toward action* and determine how you can move toward your goal.

Let's say your goal is to write a book.

Checking Facebook five times a day is not getting your book written. Talking about writing is not getting your book written. Texting your friends . . . well, you get the idea. Even joining a writers' group or going to a writers' conference isn't going to get you there. What gets you there is putting your butt in the chair and your fingers on the keyboard for extended lengths of time. You need to commit to write, even if the first draft comes out terribly.

When I set out to write this book, I began by waking up earlier so that I could get in some writing time before my wife, Ruth, awoke. Even when that meant I got very little sleep, I did it anyway. I took a few days off here and there, but they were the exception. The rule was that I was there at my computer, showing up each morning, until I had finished. I chose to make it my priority over anything that might distract me from it.

When people talk about who's stopping them from achieving their goals, it's often a critic. A family member might once have said something thoughtlessly insulting, a teacher might have given you a bad grade, a former boss might have thought you were a dunce. Yet none of these critics can actually stop you, nor do negative people deserve any spot in your path. Even if they have stolen your keyboard and broken all your pencils, they don't have any actual power to stop you.

In reality, no one's usually trying to prevent us from achieving our goals. The situation is most often one like that brilliantly portrayed in the British TV series *The Prisoner*. Throughout the series the hero, identified as Number Six, is trying to escape from evil people who are working for the villain, Number One. Finally, in the last episode he understands the answer to his question "Who is Number One?" When he first heard the answer in episode 1, it sounded like "You are Number Six." Now he understands that the answer to "Who is Number One?" is "You are, Number Six." He had metaphorically imprisoned himself. As Franz Kafka put it, "It was a barred cage that he was in. Calmly and insolently, as if at home, the din of the world streamed out and in through the bars, the prisoner was really free, he could take part in everything, nothing that went on outside escaped him, he could simply have left the cage, the bars were yards apart, he was not even a prisoner."

Even when there is a real obstacle, it is possible to get around it. Years ago my wife, Ruth, and I were traveling in India, and we changed our departure date via telephone so that we were leaving one day earlier. When we arrived at the Delhi airport at about 2:00 a.m., the guard would not let us enter the terminal because our paper ticket was for the following day. We explained that we had changed the flight date, but he wouldn't budge.

I pointed out to him that the United Airlines desk was within view, and if he allowed me to go there, I could get the date changed on my ticket and come back to show him. He refused. I offered to leave my passport with him as a guarantee. He refused. I offered to leave my wife with him as a guarantee. He refused. I offered both my wife and passport. He still refused!

Then I made a bold choice. I had seen his rifle; it looked like it was old, possibly preindependence, and likely useless. I figured the chances of it blowing up in his hands were greater than the chances of the bullet actually reaching me. So I calmly took Ruth's hand and just walked past him. He did not shoot, and I did not look back.

Most times there are no armed guards; we simply stop ourselves. We are Number One. You are responsible for deciding what you do or don't do. Don't blame others, and don't use reasons to justify or rationalize your behaviors. Although excuses may seem to get you out of difficulty at the moment, in the long run they are often counterproductive.

THE ISSUE OF TIME

One of the biggest excuses we have for not getting things done is a lack of time. We all have the same twenty-four hours in a day, and yet what Mother Teresa, Albert Einstein, Bill Gates, and Martin Luther King Jr. accomplished in their days is a lot more than what many others have.

The difference comes back to intention and attention. It's not that they had extra time; it's that they *made* time. When something is a priority in your life, you have to be willing to walk away from anything that's standing in its way. If there's something useless that's stealing your time, why are you letting it? Understanding that extra hours are not going to appear on your clock, how can you make the time to accomplish what you need to?

It may be helpful to write in a journal for a few days, noting (truthfully) what you're doing all day long and how long you spend on each task. Are you spending more time than you realized getting showered and ready in the morning, texting, e-mailing, surfing the Web, gaming? Even positive things like reading or cooking can take up too much time when you're trying to get something done. When you need to finish a report or you still haven't turned in a long application, instead of pro-crastinating and sitting around thinking about it, invoke your bias toward action by putting your normal activities aside. Get the job done. Instead of cooking, open a can. Instead of reading the newspapers, save them for later or simply toss them.

In the modern world we have an endless supply of time sink-holes. Don't fall into them. Steal back your time to support your intentions.

GETTING
UNSTUCK

CHAPTER 3

If it's not worth doing, it's not worth doing well.

—*Anonymous*

A drunk man is walking along the street and collides with a lamppost. He bounces backward, and after regaining his composure again makes his way forward, only to again collide with the same lamppost and experience a similar backward bounce. Again he regains composure, and then suffers another backward bounce. These actions are all repeated several more times. Finally, in frustration, he sits down on the ground and says, "I give up. They have me surrounded."

If we're not drunk, once we see an obstacle in our path, or experience our first bounce or two, we walk around that obstacle. Unfortunately we sometimes still have difficulty. We often think we are surrounded, and respond in the same way as the drunken guy.

So, assuming you are sober, how do you walk around obstacles?

GETTING AROUND THE LAMPPOST

The answer lies in changing the way you think about the problem. As an assignment in one of my design courses I asked each student to find something in his life that bothered him and fix it. One student, Krishna, volunteered that his bed was broken, and he could not seem to get a good night's sleep. His assignment was to solve the problem. This started a saga that lasted several weeks.

The first week Krishna reported not being able to find the correct wire to fix the frame. The second week he reported not being able to find the correct tools. The third week he was unable to find some small springs. Finally I lost patience and told him that if he did not solve the problem by the following week, he would fail. He came in the next week with a big smile on his face; I knew the drama had ended. When I called on him to report on his project, he simply said: "I bought a new bed."

It is a wonderful example of the mistake we make by working on an answer as though it were a question. Design thinking emphasizes that you always make sure you are working on the real problem. His mistake was that he originally tried to solve the wrong problem. He started by working on the question "How can I fix the bed?" The real question, of course, was "How do I get a good night's sleep?" This opened the solution space considerably and allowed a move away from the difficulties encountered in fixing the bed. Once Krishna started working on the right problem, the solution became easy: Get a new bed. This enabled him to walk around the self-imposed lamppost called "fixing the bed."

MOVING TO A HIGHER LEVEL

Have you ever had a problem you couldn't seem to solve? You probably pondered solutions over and over, maybe losing sleep. I bet you were trying to solve the wrong problem. When you can't find the answer, it is often because you are not asking the correct question.

To illustrate this, let's take the question "How might I find a spouse?"

Just because it ends with a question mark, that doesn't mean it's a question. Drop "how might I" and you get a declarative statement: "Find a spouse." This could be regarded as an answer. So we see that finding a spouse can be regarded as either an answer or a question.

What question is "Find a spouse" the answer to? There could be many. Some possibilities are:

How might I get companionship?

How might I get taken care of?

How might I stop working?

How might I have (more) sex?

How might I get my parents to stop nagging me?

How might I move to a better economic situation?

How might I improve my social life?

How might I keep up with my friends?

Each of these questions, regarded as a problem, has many possible solutions. Finding a spouse is just one possible solution to each of these. In actuality, it may not be a very good solution to any of these problems.

Experience has shown me that one of the main causes of losing sleep over a problem is that we think we are dealing with a question when in fact we are dealing with an answer (a solution) that turns out not to be a good fit to our actual problem.

A way around this dilemma is to ask, "What would it do for me if I solved this problem?" The answer to this can then be converted into a new, more generative question.

If I believe that I want a spouse to satisfy my need for companionship, the real problem (question) is "How might I find companionship?"

Finding a spouse now becomes simply one of many possible ways to find companionship. By changing the question I have altered my point of view and dramatically expanded the number of possible solutions.

The situation can be illustrated diagrammatically as:

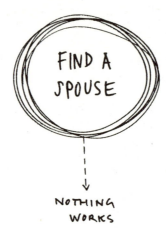

FIND A SPOUSE

NOTHING WORKS

Because I haven't been able to find a spouse thus far, I can take a different tack: I can ask what finding a spouse would do for me.

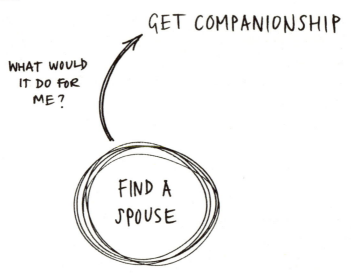

GET COMPANIONSHIP

WHAT WOULD IT DO FOR ME?

FIND A SPOUSE

I believe it would give me companionship. So the new question is "How might I get companionship?" The diagram below shows possible answers.

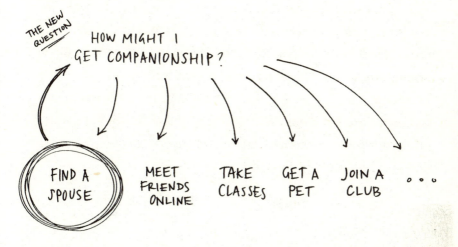

I am no longer stuck with trying to find a spouse. It's that simple.

Identifying what you expect from the solution to the problem you're stuck on brings you to a higher level and, ultimately, a better question.

Changing the question is often enough to lead to a satisfactory resolution and to make the original difficulty disappear. In this example, if I figure out how to get companionship without getting married, the issue of finding a spouse becomes moot.

This procedure can be repeated starting at the higher level. If the question of how I might find companionship becomes difficult to solve, I would ask, "What would it do for me if I found companionship?"

Possible answers might be:

I would feel less bored.

I would get social stimulation.

I would get intellectual stimulation.

I would feel less lonely.

I would feel more secure.

By choosing the one that seems most resonant (I would feel less lonely) and converting it into a question, I get a new question. "How might I feel less lonely?" is a long way from the original question: "How do I find a spouse?"

Many married people feel lonely within their marriages, so clearly even solving the original problem (finding a spouse) might not solve my actual problem of being lonely.

Now the situation looks like this:

Use this procedure whenever you find yourself stuck and losing sleep over an issue. Often it can open up a wide range of new solutions. The original problem disappears, and the way to proceed is immediately obvious.

For this to work you need to be honest enough not to hang on to the original question, no matter how comfortable you have become with hitting the lamppost. You need to be aware that there is a tendency to rationalize our dysfunctional behavior with excuses. Remember, we shy away from labeling them as excuses; instead we call them reasons. Of course, they are *goooood* reasons, right?

There isn't always a single answer to the question "How would I benefit if I had a solution to my problem?" It is simply a matter of using a different how-might-I question and repeating this procedure until you feel the *Aha!* that comes from recognizing your actual issue.

I've had students say that they felt that this method does not actually solve the original problem; it simply replaces it with one you can solve. What they do not realize is that letting go of a problem *is* often the best solution. This is especially true when you're addressing the wrong problem.

Blocks to success with this exercise happen when we can't let go of the original question. For example, in one of my workshops a woman asked, "How do I make sure my daughter gets into a good college?" She had to struggle to admit that the main payoff for her in solving this problem would be to reduce her level of anxiety. Once she made that leap, the question one level higher became "How do I become less anxious?" The new problem, at heart, was a long way from her daughter getting into a good college. In fact, it had very little to do with that. In all probability, once the daughter got into college, the mother would quickly find another issue to be anxious about. So if the mother were honest enough, she would start to work on the real problem: her anxiety.

YOUR TURN

To experience the process of walking around the lamppost, think of a problem you have been losing sleep over. This should be something that keeps bothering you and is directly related to your life, your relationships, or your job, not something abstract or global such as how to achieve world peace.

Write this item down as a short, simple how-do-I question. Then ask yourself what it would do for you if this problem were solved. In other words, if it were something that you no longer lost sleep over, what would it do for you? Write down the answer to this above your original question. Now change the answer into a question and take a few minutes to consider possible solutions to this new question.

If you are open-minded, chances are you have just walked around the lamppost.

Alternatively, let's assume you are still stuck and do not see how to solve your new problem. Now we go up one more level. Take your new question and ask yourself what it would do for you if you solved that question, and write down the answer above the new question. We now have a new question. Consider possible solutions to the newer question. You should soon realize that you just walked around another lamppost. Now, if after all this, the original problem has not disappeared or you still do not see your way clear to the solution, there is a very good chance that you are not telling yourself the truth about what the real problem is and what it would do for you if you solved it. Go back and start again!

REFRAMING

Once we are aware of a problem, we tend to plunge ahead in search of a solution, yet often we'd do better to first reconsider the question. Reframing problems can lead to much better solutions. Mental health professionals also use reframing; it is a powerful therapeutic technique. The basic idea behind reframing is to introduce a change of perspective into your thinking. This is illustrated in a variant of the classic light bulb joke:

Question: How many design thinkers does it take to change a light bulb?

Answer from a design thinker: Why use light bulbs?

There are various forms of problem statements. In the business and design thinking world they have names such as opportunity statements, how-could-we statements, and points of view.

The form I favor is point of view (POV). It is not a rigidly defined concept.[1] Its purpose is to define what a person needs—not what *we* think she needs, rather what she *actually* needs. If you want to find something new, it is important to start with a problem and not with a solution. Once you introduce solutions prematurely, you shut down the discovery process.

Reframing a problem is essentially a change of POV. At the d.school we've had several instances where reframing led to spectacular results.

Students from the "Entrepreneurial Design for Extreme Affordability" course were asked to go to Myanmar to work on a project having to do with irrigation. As part of this work they spent time with poor farmers to determine the farmers' basic problems with watering their crops. The students noticed that because there was no electricity, farmers used candles or kerosene lanterns for lighting. The students could smell the toxic fumes in the poorly ventilated farmers' huts. They also learned that candles and kerosene consumed about 25 percent of the farmers' annual income.

In some cases the farmers had old car batteries rigged to lamps so their children could do homework after dark. In these families, mothers were forced to repeatedly make tedious bike trips of several hours to get the batteries recharged. All in all, the Stanford students learned that lighting was a big issue for these farmers, so they convinced the teaching team to let them change their POV from dealing with the need for irrigation to dealing with the need for lighting.

The students developed solar-powered LED task lights that were affordable and more user-centered than alternative solar lights. They established a for-profit company called d.light that by the end of 2013 had sold over two million lights in forty-two countries. They expect to continue to grow and provide affordable solar lighting to places in the world that have either no electricity or only intermittent service. In this case it was a good thing that the students did not charge full speed ahead into the water issues. Rather, they reframed their POV to meet the needs they found on the ground.

A different type of reframing was done by students in a project named Embrace. At the request of a medical nonprofit organization, students from the "Entrepreneurial Design for Extreme Affordability" course went to Nepal to deal with problems related to incubators for premature infants. The incubators cost about $20,000 each and are equivalent to the ones used in American hospitals. The problem the students were asked to deal with was twofold: the incubators were difficult to repair locally, and power disruptions often compromised their performance. While still at Stanford the students thought in terms of battery backups and of redesigning to simplify the number of parts. Interestingly, once they got to Nepal they noticed that the usage of even the fully functioning incubators was low. The more they traveled around the country, the more they noticed that only in towns did clinics have incubators; many women living in the mountains would have great difficulty getting to them in time to save their premature infants.

The students thus reframed their POV. They realized that rather than solving the doctors' problem of keeping the incubators functional, they should be solving the mothers' problem of keeping their premature babies alive by providing the necessary warmth where and when it was needed. This led to the design of what is essentially a miniature sleeping bag with a removable pouch containing a block of waxlike material that, when heated, becomes a liquid that remains at the required temperature for nearly five hours. The heat could be supplied by boiling the pouch in water, which could be accomplished without electricity.

The device they developed sells for 1 percent of the price of the conventional incubator and offers lifesaving availability far beyond the domain of traditional incubators. The students' big breakthrough came when they realized that the initial question they were presented with—how to improve the incubators— was in fact an answer that could not work. By asking themselves what it would accomplish to have the incubator improved, they came to the real question: How could they keep babies warm enough to stay alive?

By April 2014 Embrace's infant warmers were being used in eleven different countries on three continents. The warmers provided innovative, low-cost, lifesaving technology for over fifty thousand low-birth-weight and premature infants. The number of surviving infants is increasing daily.

Reframing can also be useful in making improvements after a solution has already been found. Doug Dietz is a longtime designer of medical diagnostic equipment at GE Health Care. He had a life-changing experience when he went to a local clinic that used an MRI machine that he had designed. He introduced himself to a technologist; she told him how highly regarded his machine was, and he felt ten feet tall. Then a family appeared, trying their best to calm a screaming child. As soon as the young girl was exposed to the scary room, strangers, and the huge MRI scanner, she broke into tears and had to be sedated to hold still for the exam. Doug had no idea children were being sedated as a matter of course. When he found out that close to 85 percent of the children between three and eight years of age had to be sedated, he felt like a failure.

Shortly thereafter, while participating in a three-day intensive executive education workshop at the d.school, Doug got an insight about a shortcoming in his design process. He realized that although he had consulted widely with customer engineers, marketing people, salespeople, technologists, and doctors, he had actually never spent much time with the families and the young patients in need of the equipment he had designed.

When Doug went back to work, he consulted hospital child-life specialists, child psychologists, teachers, parents, and children. He enlisted staff from a children's museum; they spent time with kids and parents. He organized an advisory team of children who had undergone a lot of health treatments. Working with the children's museum and the children, he designed a series of MRI experiences he calls the Adventure Series.

The Adventure Series reframes the MRI experience as an adventure and not a medical procedure. Doug did this by having the rooms, floors, and MRI machines redecorated. He also developed coloring books to explain the procedure for the child at home the night before. One adventure was going away to camp and being in a tent, where if you lie very still on a sleeping bag (table) you can see the stars. Another was being in a ship lying very still, hiding from pirates.

Reframing the situation from a medical procedure into an adventure was a huge success. The child sedation rate dropped to almost nothing. Apart from the savings in time and cost, there was a notable positive difference in the experience for the children and their families. Doug reports that after their MRI examination, some children would ask their mothers when they could return to have another adventure!

The device was exactly the same; only the user experience was reframed.

These three inspirational results illustrate an important basic principle: When thinking about how to achieve your dream, don't simply charge ahead. Pause and think about what the problem really is. Go to a higher level and consider what else might be at the heart of the problem. Now reframe it. Change your point of view. Then change it again and see where you are. The real problem will reveal itself to you.

WHY IT WON'T WORK

Another useful technique for getting unstuck when you're solving a problem is one I accidentally stumbled upon when I was writing my PhD dissertation. I had completed most of my research and had been invited to present a seminar on my work at Yale University. I had given a somewhat inflated title for the seminar. The evening before the talk I started to think about my presentation and got a little nervous. I thought I should start off by coming clean about my title. I imagined myself saying,

"Although my title implies I can solve the general case, the fact is that I can only do it for special cases. I cannot solve the general case where N is any integer. The reason for this is . . ."

Then a miracle happened. As I was explaining to my imaginary audience why I could not solve the general case, it suddenly occurred to me how I could do it. I was thrilled! The next day at Yale, I gave my talk and it went well. I felt good about the presentation and the fact that I didn't have to hide behind an inaccurate title. I still think it was one of the greatest *Aha!* moments in my life.

Two important lessons emerged from this incident. The first is perhaps something you've heard before: if you get stuck while working on a problem, try putting it aside for a while. This process of mentally clearing the decks will allow your subconscious to have a crack at the problem, often resulting in new and better solutions.

The second is to take the time to explain (whether to yourself or to a friend or family member out loud) exactly why you can't solve the problem. In my case, when I explained to my phantom audience why I could not solve the general case, I was able to see that the reasons were not actually valid and that I could do it easily, using methods I knew quite well.

PREMATURE CLOSURE

When we're searching for solutions to our problems, we tend to choose the first decent idea that we come up with. Once we have an idea we feel we can fall back on, we tend to stop working hard and just go through the motions of pretending to look for better solutions—or perhaps we stop entirely. Yet this too is a form of getting stuck. We are denying ourselves the opportunity to find a more practical, elegant, or inexpensive solution.

This idea of premature closure can rear its head during any phase of any design or problem-solving process. When it occurs at the problem formation or POV generation stage, it leaves us working with the original concept for the problem statement. This severely limits the reframing, which is often the key to more effective and delightful solutions.

If it occurs during the ideation phase, it can doom the project to a mundane brute-force solution. Better results can often be obtained if more ideas are generated and used to enhance or replace the original concepts.

Consider the following problem: How do I increase my purchasing power? If I reach into my pocket and I find a dollar bill, I have a solution. If I keep looking and find a five-dollar bill, my situation has improved. Further searching might reveal a twenty. If I am lucky, upon opening another compartment in my wallet I find a blank check and maybe various credit cards. Now I have a lot of options to choose from, and I could combine or use any single one that I feel is best for the given circumstances. Either way, I have come a long way from my first solution—a single dollar bill.

The proper state of mind is one that welcomes each subsequent solution with as much joy as the first one, and then puts each aside and keeps looking. Ultimately you'll face restrictions that will end the solution-seeking process. You'll run out of time. You'll run out of resources. Or you'll find the solution that you're sure is exactly the right one and no longer be tempted by the challenge to find something better.

WHAT WE DON'T HAVE

One spring day I was riding my bicycle in Death Valley when I came upon an astonishing sight. A section of the roadway was covered with thousands of dead caterpillars squashed flat by cars as they attempted to cross the road. Looking more closely, I could see masses of caterpillars on each side slowly making their way toward the road. There were as many on the left side of the road headed to the right side as there were on the right side headed toward the left.

This was barren country, and as far as I could make out, the landscape was identically empty on both sides of the road. What motivated the caterpillars to cross? I have no idea! Probably entomologists have a *goooood* reason. Yet the memory has stayed with me as a constant reminder of analogous, meaningless dysfunctional behaviors in my life. How many times have I crossed a road pointlessly when staying where I was would have been fine?

Like those caterpillars, we are often more interested in what we do not have than in what we have. We may strive for something, and the effort may consume us. Once we have obtained our goal, it tends to lose its hold on us, and we are off to the next pursuit. Currently in America, approximately 50 percent of marriages end in divorce. Many of these are followed by remarriages. We are always looking for something different, something better.

People change jobs because they get bored. They travel not for the joy of traveling but simply to get away. It is common for people traveling to other cities and countries to visit museums, even though they never bother to go to the ones in their own hometowns. In some people's lives there is constant change for change's sake, like the caterpillars crossing the road to reach an identical piece of Death Valley real estate. Maybe going from one place to another does no harm, or maybe you get flattened while you are crossing the road.

Some professions have motivation for road-crossing behavior

built in. In sports there is always the next game and the next season to work toward. In research there is the next project and the next paper, always more knowledge to achieve. In school, there is always the next exam, class, and term. Then there are the various levels to graduate from: grade school, junior high school, high school, college, and graduate school. In jobs we work our way up the ladder, always looking ahead. In these examples, at least, there seems to be something bigger and better on the other side of the road.

In all these examples you will see that what has been left behind was at one point something you desired most in life. Yet now it hardly matters to you. There is nothing wrong with change and moving forward in life if it gets you to a better spot. Unfortunately, all too often in our search for the next big thing we don't take the time to appreciate the satisfaction of achieving a goal, or the process itself. We are so busy being enticed by our next endeavor that we forget to savor what is already there and could be deeply meaningful. It is useful to remember the adage "The more things change, the more they remain the same."

A good case in point comes from a colleague of mine who made some important discoveries and became very prominent in the area of applied mathematics. Periodically he would win some award or receive an honorary degree. Invariably he would tell me about the next honor he was hoping for. Then, when he got it, he would tell me he was pleased because he could use it to get a pay raise in the coming year. In fact, he was unmarried, very well paid, and had no need of extra income. In spite of his many successes and his many raises, he was basically an unhappy person. Sadly, he reminded me of the caterpillars, always hoping to find something on the other side of the road, although it was all around him already on his side of the road.

Often the things we strive for only represent more of something we already have: money, fame, appreciation, love. It's an endless chase; as the saying goes, You can't get enough from more. For some people it's the thrill of the chase that they really enjoy, so once they get what they have been seeking, it becomes irrelevant. There's nothing inherently wrong with this, as long as you are honest with yourself about your goals. Otherwise you are bound to spend your life frustrated and unhappy, like my friend.

There is an ethos regarding change in Silicon Valley. Within many companies there is always a fierce struggle to develop something new in an effort to stay ahead of competitors. Silicon Valley people believe their companies will stagnate and die without continual innovation: it's the ultimate what-have-you-done-lately? culture. To maintain status in such a culture, people always need a new and evolving story. If they don't deliver, they feel they lose face. These people are under a lot of pressure, and in their desperation they sometimes act like those caterpillars, taking their organizations on meaningless road-crossing journeys in pursuit of a new story to tell their friends.

The moral is that change for change's sake is not necessarily good. Sometimes it is okay to fail in the pursuit of a meaningful goal. But it is never okay to commit organizational suicide just to save face with your friends or impress your latest love interest.

TWENTY-TWO WAYS TO GET UNSTUCK

Once you have a problem statement, there are many formal methods that can assist you in generating solutions.[2] Moreover, as you move forward in the problem-solving process, it is important to keep in mind that all problem statements (including POVs) are best regarded as provisional. Subsequent work often leads to multiple revisions of the problem statement.

Often just getting a good problem statement is enough to set you on the road to a great solution. At other times a satisfying direction is not apparent, and frustration sets in. My dear friend Rolf Faste created the handout that follows for our creativity workshops, listing twenty-two things to try if you find yourself hitting the lamppost. I have never lost my admiration for Rolf's incredible ability to use simple sketches to bring complex ideas to life. In only one page he succeeded in beautifully summarizing the major tools from the product design culture that developed into the design thinking movement. (The following two pages each formed one column on the original 8.5" x 11" handout.)

Rolf's drawing is supplemented by my short explanation about each of the items. It is useful to master a few of these methods.

Hard Work

This is my most productive technique. Sometimes things come to me in a flash. But most of the time the flash is preceded by a lot of hard work and frustration. There are no magic methods that substitute for *attention* and *intention.*

Create a Supportive Environment

Take time to unclutter your work area, and keep supportive supplies handy. Make your surroundings remarkable and stimulating. Abraham Verghese had a poster printed, saying that the book he was working on had won a Nobel Prize and been on the *New York Times* best-seller list for over a year. He did not get the Nobel, but the other part came true.

Relax

To allow your subconscious to do its work, you must relax. There are many stories of people having breakthroughs during

Integration of Creativity into the ME Curriculum

REVIEW OF CREATIVE STRATEGIES

① HARD WORK { USUALLY COMES FIRST   MOST OF THE STRATEGIES
               LISTED ARE MOST USEFUL WHEN YOU ARE "BLOCKED"

② CREATE A SUPPORTIVE ENVIRONMENT   INVEST
                                                      IN
                                                      YOURSELF

③ RELAX   EVEN   DREAM   TAP YOUR SUBCONSCIOUS

④ BRAINSTORMING EXPRESS TEST CYCLE

DEFER JUDGMENT   PIGGYBACK

GOALS: A FLUENCY : QUANTITY
        B FLEXIBILITY : VARIETY   LEAPFROG

⑤ LISTS
⑥ META-LISTS → LISTS OF THINGS TO MAKE LISTS OF !

⑦ MORPHOLOGICAL   POWER   TIMING
   ANALYSIS: MATCHING UP   SOURCE   MECH   INDICATOR
                  ATTRIBUTE LISTS

⑧ IDEA LOGS ✛ DRAWING: TANGIBLE
                          SPECULATION

⑨ HUMOR
⑩ CONVERSATION

⑪ FORCED TRANSFORMATIONS
   CHECKLIST SOLITARE   MAGNIFY   MINIFY ƎSЯƎVƎЯ
                                          ↙ COMBINE

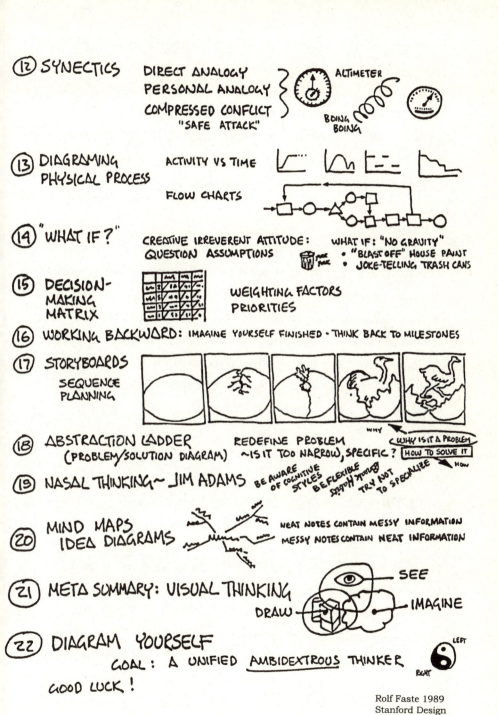

(12) SYNECTICS
DIRECT ANALOGY
PERSONAL ANALOGY
COMPRESSED CONFLICT
"SAFE ATTACK"

ALTIMETER

BOING BOING

(13) DIAGRAMING PHYSICAL PROCESS
ACTIVITY VS TIME

FLOW CHARTS

(14) "WHAT IF?"
CREATIVE IRREVERENT ATTITUDE:
QUESTION ASSUMPTIONS

WHAT IF: "NO GRAVITY"
• "BLAST OFF" HOUSE PAINT
• JOKE-TELLING TRASH CANS

(15) DECISION-MAKING MATRIX
WEIGHTING FACTORS
PRIORITIES

(16) WORKING BACKWARD: IMAGINE YOURSELF FINISHED • THINK BACK TO MILESTONES

(17) STORYBOARDS
SEQUENCE PLANNING

(18) ABSTRACTION LADDER
(PROBLEM/SOLUTION DIAGRAM)
REDEFINE PROBLEM
~IS IT TOO NARROW, SPECIFIC?
WHY
WHY IS IT A PROBLEM
HOW TO SOLVE IT

(19) NASAL THINKING ~ JIM ADAMS
BE AWARE OF COGNITIVE STYLES
BE FLEXIBLE
TRY NOT TO SPECIALIZE
HOW

(20) MIND MAPS
IDEA DIAGRAMS
NEAT NOTES CONTAIN MESSY INFORMATION
MESSY NOTES CONTAIN NEAT INFORMATION

(21) META SUMMARY: VISUAL THINKING
SEE
IMAGINE
DRAW

(22) DIAGRAM YOURSELF
GOAL: A UNIFIED AMBIDEXTROUS THINKER
LEFT
RIGHT
GOOD LUCK!

Rolf Faste 1989
Stanford Design

their dreams and daydreams. My favorite has to do with the Irish astronomer and mathematician W. R. Hamilton, who was walking with his wife when the solution to a long-standing problem popped into his head.[3] History does not say if his wife knew he was daydreaming while supposedly spending time with her. Without exposing the details—which might put my marriage in jeopardy—I can affirm that this method works.

Brainstorming

In the Stanford product design program, students are taught to use a problem-solving process (we called it a design process) with the acronym ETC. The first step is to *express* an idea: come up with a trial solution. The next step is to *test* the idea: see what about it works and what does not. The third step is to *cycle*: use what you have learned to come up with a modified or new idea—that is, something new to express. This is repeated until you have a solution you are proud of—or until you run out of time.

In general, the *express* part of the process is generative. Your attitude here should be one of optimism about your idea. In contrast, when you get to the *test* part of the process, you need to change attitude and become a skeptic. Push yourself to find out what needs to be changed. In this way you need to flip attitudes as you cycle from express to test and from test to express. Two major tools are useful in this process: one is brainstorming, and the other is prototyping.

Brainstorming is perhaps the most familiar of all the methods in the diagram. Sometimes the word is used to simply describe a person coming up with ideas. In our context it refers to a more formal procedure through which a group of people gather to deal with a specific issue. The object is to come up with many varied ideas. (We call this fluency and flexibility.) Ideally, a brainstorming group is chosen that represents enough variety of experience and knowledge that people can naturally build on each other's ideas (piggybacking), and also jump to completely new ideas (leapfrogging).

Brainstorming sessions are not supposed to be evaluative. They are meant to open up possibilities, no matter how far-fetched. Thus a basic rule is to *defer judgment* during the session. This is a somewhat unfortunate phrase, implying as it does that the judgmental hammer will soon come crashing down. A better description of the participants' desired state during a brainstorming session would be *gleefully accepting.* Wild ideas are encouraged. Usually a recorder or facilitator monitors the session to make sure people stay on the topic and that there are no cross-conversations (the rule is, one conversation at a time!).

Brainstorming in a group has the advantage of getting you out of your own head and letting you build on the ideas of others. Some people are loners and do not need others. (I have a friend who is a great designer who hates brainstorming. He tells me he gets his best ideas during long, solitary jogs through the mountains.) Obviously, most of us can profit from other people's ideas. Diversity of backgrounds can lead to solutions that we might not arrive at on our own.

Lists

A list is a very simple and useful problem-solving tool. As the word implies, just make a list of all the possibilities. The trick is in generating a list inclusive enough to move you toward a solution. When Paul graduated from college, he decided he would figure out his future by using lists. First, he made a list of all the things he wanted out of his career. He listed things like "Be my own boss," "Use my engineering training," "Do some public relations," "Use my drawing ability," "Travel," "Have time for my family," and "Be located in the San Francisco Bay Area."

Although the list was longer than this, you get the idea. It led him to a part of the solution: he needed to own a business producing something for which he could be involved in all aspects—especially development, production, marketing, advertisement, and sales. The next step was to find a product to build this business around. Again, Paul used lists. This time he copied out the names of every type of product in the yellow pages. He spent a long time going over each product and thinking about whether it would be something he could build a business around, and which would satisfy his criteria in the original list of what he wanted out of his career.

Using this process, he found an unlikely product: a secret recipe for beef jerky. It turned out to be incredibly successful, both making a large financial profit and satisfying everything on his career list.

Meta-lists

These are lists that contain the names of things from which to make more detailed lists. For example, you make a list of places to visit and then separate lists of things to do for each place.

Morphological Analysis

This is the process of matching up elements from different columns of attribute lists. For example, if we want to design a clock, we could make a column listing power sources (for instance, batteries, AC, mechanical, solar, water), a column listing timing mechanisms (gears, escapements, vibrations, pendulum), and a column listing indicators (two hands, three hands, LEDs, digital wheels). By forming all possible combinations of these elements, we automatically generate a large number of alternatives for clock designs. When attribute lists have many items, this method lends itself very nicely to computer implementation.

Idea Logs

These are notebooks in which you sketch out your ideas, using drawings, words, and even pasted-in items to create a record of tangible speculations on your part. It is good to develop the habit of creating notebooks in which to record your ideas. Without a record, ideas are often forgotten and lost forever. The most famous idea logs ever created were the notebooks of Leonardo da Vinci. I have found many lesser mortals can also profit by using this tool. Unlike Leonardo, however, many people actually get a lot of things from their idea logs implemented during their lifetimes.

Humor

This is a great idea-generation tool. Even for very serious problems, joking around can get you where serious thought is afraid to go.

Conversation

Some people are very secretive about their problems, and consequently they are often on their own. It is not a healthy psychological state to be in, and often not very productive. There are countless stories about how, in the famous "idea factories" of Bell Labs, Building 20 at MIT, and various Silicon Valley companies, casual conversation led to a big breakthrough. Talking to people is a great way to stimulate ideas.

Forced Transformations

This is the process of purposefully modifying your ideas to make the conventional into the unconventional. Alex Osborn, the famous early creativity guru, created a checklist of possible modifications, with items such as *magnify* and *minimize*, which referred to changing the scale of an idea. This method can be extended to include any type of transformation. For example, you can combine two unrelated ideas, such as "fish" and "tower." If you make yourself a deck of cards in which each card lists a single transformation, you can generate a lot of ideas all by yourself by simply following the transformation on each card. If you lay the cards end to end, it looks a little like a game of solitaire.[4]

Synectics

This term, derived from the Latin *synectica*, means "the joining together of different and apparently irrelevant elements." In this context it stands for the use of analogy to come up with solutions. The method calls for thinking of situations or items analogous to what you are working on in the hope that the analogy will reveal a better idea. It is useful to consider analogies that are directly related to the situation under consideration and also analogies that are personally related to the problem solver. Another useful concept in the synectics framework is the *compressed conflict*, a combination of two concepts that seem contradictory. "Safe attack," for example, one such combination, was central to the development of the concept of vaccines: by using a *safe* dose we *attack* the body with a mild case of a disease so that it produces antibodies that will protect it. Thinking of the problem along these seemingly contradictory lines opens new avenues to us.

Diagraming Physical Process

This is a tool used to distill problems to their essence. For some types of problems, idea generation can be aided by plotting some performance variable against time or another variable, or by drawing flow charts that represent an entire process.

"What If?"

This is a great way to start a question during idea generation. What if there was no gravity? What if there was blast-off house paint? What if there was a joke-telling trash can? These questions, by taking us off the main track, create an irreverent attitude that leads us to question assumptions about the problem.

Decision-Making Matrix

This is a good way to compare different ideas, by creating a matrix in which the rows represent the different ideas and the columns represent attributes within these ideas. For example, in choosing a bride, Kumar labeled each row with the name of a different candidate and each column with an attribute such as education, appearance, wealth, or family. Assigning a number to each matrix element transforms the comparison to a quantitative measure. Adding all the numbers in a row gives a total score for that idea. Also, weighting factors can be used to prioritize certain attributes.

Working Backward

Imagine that the problem has been solved, and then work back to the beginning. This way you can see what all the milestones are. If nothing else, this method is great for scheduling.

Storyboards

These aids for sequential planning are well known in the movie industry. They can be used anytime you want to tell a story in a linear manner. They are, in fact, a very pictorial version of the *journey map*, a diagram showing a linear sequence of events.

How-Why Diagram

This diagram can be used to redefine a problem, much like our method for changing the question (see "Moving to a Higher Level" earlier in this chapter). The idea is to generate a diagram showing a string of causes and effects. For a given problem the diagram lists a way of doing something—the *how*—and then *why* it is done. A lot of ideas can be generated this way. There are many variants, such as the how-why-why diagram, or the why-why-why diagram.

These diagrams are loosely related to the *abstraction ladder*, which is based on S. I. Hayakawa's ladder of four levels of linguistic abstraction.[5] The bottom level consists of concrete things: swimming goggles, a telephone, a mug, and so on. On the next level, there are *groups* of concrete things: schoolchildren, power tools, cars, livestock. The third level consists of broader groups: women, men, movies, communication devices, decorations. At the top level, there are more abstract concepts: communism, power, fairness, success, good, evil.

By diagramming the levels of abstraction for the problem/solution, you are better able to see if you are working too narrowly, being too specific—in which case you might want to redefine the problem.

Nasal Thinking

This is my colleague Jim Adams's term for the use of different cognitive styles. The idea is to be flexible in the way you look at things. Try to imagine what you would do if you thought with your nose or tried not to speak. In this way you "see" your problem differently and open up new solution ideas. Adams's classic book *Conceptual Blockbusting* contains a lot of other tools for overcoming blocks to creative problem solving.

Mind Maps

These *relationship maps* diagram the connections between pieces of information in a nonlinear manner supposed to be analogous to the way your brain stores information. Mind maps are great for providing a broad understanding of how diverse parts relate to the whole. Before the widespread use of computers, most information was stored linearly. Now we all do computer searches in nonlinear ways. This gives us an experiential understanding of the saying "Neat notes contain messy information; messy notes contain neat information."

To make a mind map, start at the center of your space and write a word or short phrase that will be the main topic. Then see what other idea (word) this evokes and write it a short distance away. Connect the two words with a line. Next, go back to the first word and see what else it evokes. Write this new word in another direction and connect a line to it from the first word.

Keep repeating this process until you run out of ideas. Then, use each of the secondary words as a root, and repeat the entire process. Of course, I have explained this in too linear a manner, and the words in the map can be generated in any order the connections come to mind. The following figure shows a mind map created by David Kelley. The first entry was "the d-School @ STANFORD." The map was for generating ideas related to designing the Stanford d.school.

Meta Summary

This is a tool for what is sometimes called *visual thinking*. Here we approach a problem using our visual abilities to see, draw, and imagine. We can generate new ideas by drawing things that we see and things that we imagine. We seek solutions by bringing together results from these different aspects of visual thinking. The overlap among different aspects is represented graphically by a Venn diagram, in which each aspect is shown as a circle, and our attention is called to the ideas in the area where the interiors of all the circles overlap.

Diagram Yourself

In this method you examine your own problem-solving process and strive to make it *ambidextrous*, meaning that you use both right-brain and left-brain activities equally. In one variant of self-diagramming, one person lies down on a long sheet of rolled-out paper, on which another draws around his body to make an outline. Then the first person labels each part of this body outline with comic-strip-type balloons containing whatever terms come to mind, thus balancing the intellectual/verbal with the emotional/visual. In Chinese terms, you are striving for balance between *yin* and *yang*.

IN MY VIEW IT is not useful to jump from method to method. Instead it is better to become adept at a few problem-solving strategies and stick with those. The more you practice your chosen techniques, the more easily you can unblock yourself at will.

FINDING "" ASSISTANCE

CHAPTER 4

If you always do what you've always done,
you'll always get what you've always gotten.

—Anthony Robbins

When it comes to achieving what you want in life, it's rare that you can do it entirely on your own. Often you'll need a little assistance from your friends. It's said that it's not *what* you know but *who* you know. I agree with that, though in its less cynical form: we are all better off when we assist each other to figure things out.

LEARNING FROM EVERYONE

I have found colleagues to be sources of enduring wisdom. My colleague Tom taught me—as well as his students—that we don't have enough time to hurry. This means that when you do things in a rush, you are invariably going to mess up. It will take you more time to clean up the mess than if you took the time to do it right. Tom's advice always comes to mind when I am fumbling with my key in a futile effort to speed up the bike-locking process so I can rush to an appointment.

My colleague Henry left an indelible impression on me one afternoon as we were biking home together. I excitedly told him I had just made a great research discovery. He asked, "Is it good enough that you can describe it before we reach my turnoff at the next corner?" Unfortunately, it wasn't.

Henry also told me something that one of the kings of England said to his son: "Whenever you get a chance to either sit down or go to the toilet, take it, because you never know when your next chance will arise." The wisdom behind that advice became clear when I sat in an auditorium with a thousand other people, waiting uncomfortably for a very embarrassed famous author to return after having interrupted his reading midsentence to use the bathroom. I have found that this royal advice works especially well for teachers.

One of the most important things I have learned from colleagues is how *not* to be. I had a colleague who was basically a nice person; I never experienced anything except kindness from him. Sadly, though, he treated a junior staff member who worked directly for him shabbily, forcing the staffer to move to a different university. After seeing this, I resolved to be especially concerned with treating younger colleagues fairly. An administrator once told me I was "a reverse ass-kisser," meaning that I treated underlings with more deference than I did my supervisors. I took that as a compliment.

The fact is, we can choose to learn from others. We can emulate their positive attributes and guard against their negative ones. We can learn from a child as well as from a famous celebrity. It is important not to be disillusioned when you find out your idols have clay feet. They can still be your teachers. You might even be able to learn more from obviously imperfect people than from those still pretending to be perfect.

Does the fact that Mahatma Gandhi was not a great father to his children invalidate his message and example? Does the fact that a politician had an illicit affair invalidate the good work she has done? You can choose a priori to rule certain influences out of your life, or you can be inclusive and take the relevant lessons from each. I believe the latter course leads to a richer life experience.

CUTTING OTHERS DOWN

I was part of a ten-person teaching team leading a weeklong intensive workshop in the d.school that we called Summer College. Five members of the team were always present. The others came as needed. The participants were PhD and master's students from different departments at Stanford. It was a wonderful experience for all, and the students always gave it the highest possible ratings; many said it was the best experience in their university careers.

The students always commented on how they had never before seen such collegiality among faculty. They were inspired by the fact that five faculty members were always there with them, and that we clearly enjoyed being with each other. For many it was a refreshing change from the world of backbiting and one-upmanship in which they were mired during their thesis research.

Many students live in a world where people think they make themselves bigger by making their colleagues smaller. However, if you bad-mouth a colleague, you actually make yourself smaller, not larger. For example, if I tell you how wonderful the people I work with are, by association you have to think I am pretty good too. On the other hand, if I tell you about my colleagues' defects, by association it makes me seem a little less admirable. Unfortunately these dysfunctional attitudes are not limited to universities. They are fixtures in many families and in most organizations.

Consider how it feels if, every time you go for a haircut, the hairdresser spends the whole time telling you how bad all the other local hairdressers are—they don't know what they're doing, they fry people's hair, they charge too much. Eventually you will start to wonder why your hairdresser feels such a need to cut others down. Obviously she's concerned about losing out to the competition, which may make you wonder if she has good reason to feel so threatened.

For you to succeed—even to win a job or a promotion over someone else—does not require you to cut down the other person. If anything, complimenting your rival shows class. Just work on yourself; be concerned with your own strengths and qualifications, and don't worry about what your competitors are up to.

MENTORING

A lot of fuss is made over the formal mentoring process, yet I'm not convinced it's very helpful. What I prefer, instead, are mini-mentorships. While working on this book, for instance, I asked everyone I knew who had published a book for advice. That way I had a whole team of advisers, each with a different experience and perspective to share.

Don't be shy about doing this, provided you're open to the idea of doing the same for someone in return. You never know what you're going to learn or who will be helpful as you set out on a new pursuit. People can surprise you; sometimes the ones you're sure are generous will be stingy with their advice because they fear competition, and the ones you least expect will come through for you in a big way.

It's okay to ask for assistance. Look for people in your life who have accomplished things that you want to accomplish, and talk to them about how they did it and what they would do differently if they had it to do over. Get feedback from as many people as you can. You don't need to follow all or even most of it. Keep in mind that the more input you get, the more you have to sift through for gems.

GOOD ARTISTS COPY; GREAT ARTISTS STEAL

Steve Jobs often mentioned that he believed "good artists copy; great artists steal," a quote he attributed to Pablo Picasso. There's no evidence that Picasso ever said that, but many people give him credit for it anyway. In 1920 T. S. Eliot wrote, "Immature poets imitate; mature poets steal; bad poets deface what they take, and good poets make it into something better, or at least something different."

The truth is, there's very little new under the sun. As my colleague Larry Leifer says, "All design is redesign." Everything you can think of has at least in part been thought of before, and it would be stupid to ignore the wisdom of the people who've preceded you. If you see good information and you don't use it, you're just being silly. Nobody can survive on his own; the fact that you know how to speak, how to read, how to add, it's all because you've taken someone else's idea and used it for your own needs. Society depends on building on other people's ideas.

So don't be too concerned about "stealing." Of course, don't take credit for someone else's work or simply copy something outright without improving it or putting your own spin on it. Understand that it's okay to build off others' ideas, and don't be too possessive of your own.

It's disturbing to realize that lives might have been saved if some researchers weren't so secretive and fixed on winning the race to a Nobel Prize. Some people are fiercely protective of their own data and ideas, often for years, until they can publish their work. The public good would be much better served if people worked more collaboratively.

Commit yourself to radical collaboration.

THE CURSE OF NETWORKING

If you read business books or take classes, you've undoubtedly been told about the power of networking—handing out your business card at social luncheons, showing up at key events, and promoting yourself. It's so smarmy and manipulative, and usually pretty transparent.

My best advice for you is not to network at all. If what you're really doing is trying to buddy up to people you think are on a higher plane than you are to get help from them, it's a lecherous relationship and it's not genuine. There are expert networkers who succeed at whatever they're trying to promote. Even so, when I go to sleep at night I'm glad I'm me and not them.

I've heard several cautionary tales of people who've overstepped the privileges of acquaintance. Never pretend that you have a relationship with someone that goes beyond what's really there. An opportunistic person might say, "Joe Smith suggested I contact you," when in fact Joe Smith said no such thing. When this gets back to Joe, can you guess what he's going to say? Don't assume it's okay to use someone's name to get in the door, even if you consider that person a friend. Ask first, or it's likely to backfire.

Life is not about using other people as you climb to the top. Stay real, instead, and build friendships. Too many people are afraid to mix their business lives with their personal lives, and I think that's sad. That came to me once when I was talking with Jean and Georges, who'd worked together for years, and I realized they barely knew anything about each other. They'd never been in each other's homes, and they didn't know anything about each other's spouses or children. What a waste. Don't be afraid of real human relationships. They matter.

Some people have bad experiences working with their friends. Yet there are many examples of lifelong friend/work connections. My colleague David Kelley realized, when he was still a Stanford master's student, that it was fun to work with his friends. He formed a company called Intergalactic Design with several of his classmates. Three companies and over forty years later, some of the same friends are still working with him.

It is common wisdom that if you lend money to your friends, you will lose both your money and your friendship. I guess that is the case if you have the wrong friends. I have always found it a great pleasure to assist friends to fund their projects or meet temporary needs, and I have never lost my money or my friendships.

When you forge these kinds of real relationships, the word *networking* doesn't even come into play. You naturally think of each other when opportunities arise. You ask for assistance and they show up, because they are friends and that's what friends do, not because you gave them a fake smile and a firm handshake at a luncheon.

Let people see you as human. Be real. Ask yourself, Who would you rather see at your door, a friend or a door-to-door salesman?

Be proactive in making friendships wherever you land. Invite people out to eat or over to your house. When you hear that a loved one of theirs is sick, follow up and ask about it the next day.

YOUR TURN

Do you have coworkers you don't know much about? Take time to get to know some of them. Make a few casual lunch or coffee dates, and take time to have a social (not business, or office gossip) conversation. Find out about their lives, and if they are interested, share information about yours.

WHAT IT COMES DOWN to is that if you want people to assist you, you should (a) *ask* them, because not everyone is that attuned to what you need, and (b) be a decent human being. Do not pretend you know more than you do. Most people are flattered when you have a genuine need and ask for their expertise. When you're offered assistance, respect others' time constraints—don't call every day, or expect them to write responses to a hundred questions—and be appreciative.

DOING

IS

everything

CHAPTER 5

For the things we have to learn before we can do them,
we learn by doing them.

—*Aristotle*

Whenever anyone makes an important change, it's because a switch has flipped. Someone who has struggled her whole life with her weight finally decides to get fit. Someone who has put up with an abusive boss for years finally has enough and quits. Someone who has harbored a secret crush finally takes the plunge and asks her beloved out for coffee. A shift has happened that has made action favorable to inaction.

You can sit around in the dark waiting for the light to come on, or you can get up, walk across the room, and flip the switch yourself.

TRYING AND DOING

As we've established, there is a big difference between *trying* to do something and actually *doing* it. They're two totally different actions. The difficulty arises when people conflate them.

If you *try* to do something, it may or may not happen. If

it does not happen, you might try using an altered strategy, and again it may not happen. Although this could go on indefinitely, usually it lasts until you luck out and succeed, get tired of trying, or get distracted by something else. Clearly this is a very unproductive way to go about your life.

If you are *doing* something, then no matter how many times you hit a barrier, or how frustrated your original strategy becomes, you intend to get the job done, and you bring to bear on it the inner resolve and attention necessary to fulfill your intention.

Doing takes *intention* and *attention*.

Remember the exercise I gave my students in which I asked one of them first to *try* to take an object from me, and then to actually *take* the object from me? Wrestling over the object when the volunteer is trying is often fun for both of us. Trying can often be fun and easy. Nevertheless it is *doing* that gets things done.

In 1974 I was having lunch with my friend Harold in the Russian Tea Room, a fashionable restaurant near Carnegie Hall in New York City. The waiters in this restaurant all wear Russian Cossack uniforms, which my friend admired because he was a big fan of the Soviet Union. The thought came to me, as he kept expressing this admiration, how wonderful it would be to get Harold one of these uniforms. Suddenly I just decided I would do it. I didn't know how, yet whatever it took I *would* give him one of these uniforms as a present.

Taking advantage of Harold's legendary frugality, I told him that I would pay for the lunch if he would go get the car. I sized up all the waiters as soon as he left, choosing the one who looked most amenable to a beneficial economic transaction. I called that waiter to my table, told him how much we had enjoyed the lunch, and relayed Harold's great admiration for the uniform. I told him that if he could get me a uniform, I would make it worth his while.

"How worthwhile?" he asked.

I took out my wallet, opened it to the billfold section, and said, "You decide." He removed a $10 bill (which would be $50 in today's money) and left without another word. A short time later I was waiting by the curb with a full uniform, including boots, wrapped in a day-old newspaper.

Harold died in 2011, and I often think of him when I'm doing the trying-versus-doing demonstration. I recall that moment of triumph and the resulting flash of insight that I gained long ago. I am still warmed by recalling how happy and astounded Harold was when I gave him the uniform.

Another time I was leading a workshop for a professional group in Seoul, Korea. A young woman volunteered to do the trying-versus-doing exercise, and when I asked her to take the object from my hands, she immediately seized my eyeglasses and threatened to break them unless I gave her the object. I paid the ransom, and retrieved my glasses unharmed. It was, perhaps, a bit scary, yet she certainly had a creative approach!

This incident brings up the question of ethics and morality. Here's an extreme case: if I had to kill you to move from trying to doing, in normal circumstances I would change my mind and decide not to do it. The exercise is about the difference between trying and doing. It is not about ethics or morality. You need to decide for yourself if you are going to violate any boundaries. If doing requires trespassing, then perhaps it is time to change your intention from doing to not doing.

I do not know if the woman would have broken my glasses. Given her previous behavior, I think there is a good chance she would have carried out her threat. If she had broken them, I could have had a new pair made. In any case, her intention was strong enough to get her the object, and in my view no strong ethical or moral boundaries were crossed.

Recently I had a family experience that beautifully illustrates the difference between trying and doing. My wife, Ruth, and I were in San Francisco for the evening. After dinner, driving past the Roxie—a neighborhood movie theater we occasionally frequent—I noticed a crowd and a program that sounded interesting to me. I suggested that Ruth should buy the tickets while I hunted for a parking place. She was lukewarm about the movie, yet agreed to the plan anyway.

When I returned to the Roxie ten minutes later, I was shocked to find that Ruth was not in line. She told me that she had tried to buy tickets but they were sold out. Because I really wanted to go, I sprang into action: I went to the box office and asked the seller if there were any cancellations; she agreed to take my name, and I agreed to wait close by. Then I started to ask people in the line if they had an extra ticket. I was able to purchase one ticket from someone approaching the box office for a refund and another one from someone in the line whose friend had phoned to say she was not coming. Suddenly we were *doing*.

This incident illustrates some basic points. My wife did not really want to go to the movie, and when they told her that the show was sold out, she had a *goooood* reason for not going. I was determined to go. So the fact that they were sold out was simply a lamppost I had to walk around. I knew the "sold out" reason was bullshit. The moral: If you don't really want to do it, then the world might be nice enough to give you *goooood* reasons why it can't be done. If you really want to do it, those reasons are not going to stop you.

Actually, in this case we would have been much better off trying rather than doing. The movie and live show were terrible. As they say, be careful what you wish for.

We can also apply the notion of trying and doing to a person, rather than her actions. Instead of trying, you would see yourself as a trier; instead of doing, you would see yourself as a doer. Unless you are an extreme type A personality, you will have a better life incorporating both trier and doer into your self-image and calling on each as appropriate. Come to think of it, maybe you should incorporate both *especially* if you are type A—a little more trying and a little less doing might extend your life span.

AFFIRMATIONS: A TOOL FOR CHANGE?

Maxwell Maltz was a cosmetic surgeon who found that his patients were often not satisfied with their surgery, even though it was technically successful. He believed this was in large measure due to the patients having unhealthy self-images. His solution was to develop a series of techniques with which he felt people could improve their self-images.

One of his methods was to have a person set a series of goals and then picture achieving them with the aid of mental visualization techniques. Maltz relied on the power of self-affirmation and mental visualizations as well as the connection between the mind and the body. In 1960 he published his ideas in *Psycho-Cybernetics*, a straightforward self-help book that ultimately sold more than thirty million copies. A large industry and volumes of literature subsequently developed around the use of affirmations as a tool to change self-image. Several of my students found Maltz's affirmation exercises useful.

An affirmation is a carefully formatted statement that you

repeat frequently to yourself, and which can also be written down. People who perform affirmations contend that a positive mental attitude supported by affirmations will make almost anything possible. For an affirmation to be effective, they believe, it needs to be present-tense, positive, personal, and specific. You pick something you want to change or reinforce, and take time each day to tell yourself that it has happened. To use an affirmation to improve your self-image, for example, you might repeat to yourself, "I am a loving person when I'm interacting with my daughter."

Certainly a positive mental attitude is a big plus in life. Affirmations work well for some people—however they're not for everybody. I find it hard to convince myself that the positive stuff is really true. It reminds me of the part in the film *Snow White and the Seven Dwarfs* where the wicked queen is daily asking the magic mirror, "Who is the fairest in the land?" Even though the queen gets the answer she wants, she does not seem to believe it. If she did, she wouldn't need to keep going back to the mirror to check.

To me, the problem with the self-affirmation movement is that people often feel that positive affirmations seem false, yet they readily accept the negative self-images they carry around as true. It is a classic example of seeing a glass as half empty or half full. For many of us, the half empty seems real, and the half full seems false. Probably the glass is both half full and half empty, and we get to decide which way we see it. The idea is to get enough external verification of the half-full version that our self-image really changes, and we do not need to keep going back to the magic mirror in our heads to find out who and what we are.

One way to do this is to use affirmations in a slightly indirect way. Instead of dealing directly with a desired accomplishment, we can use affirmations to modify a behavior such that the modified behavior leads indirectly to the desired accomplishment.

For example, in one study students with low academic self-esteem were not asked to think of themselves differently; instead they were simply asked to list and write about characteristics they felt were positive in regard to education and career preparation. These students ended staying in school at much higher rates than those in a peer group.

This is closely related to the advice parents and teachers are often given, to affirm their children's efforts rather than their accomplishments. The idea is that if affirmations are given, they should reinforce the desired characteristic—namely, the effort, which then endures and transcends any transitory failure. When reinforcement is based solely on accomplishment, it doesn't foster the resiliency that is needed to overcome life's inevitable disappointments.

JUST DO IT

When I started teaching the course on which some of this book is based, I knew that I wanted students to choose projects having to do with their own lives. Moreover, I had met a lot of engineers in Silicon Valley who worked for big companies, such as Hewlett-Packard, and had dreams of starting their own companies. This was back in the 1960s, before the availability of serious angel and venture funds or the strong culture of start-ups.

People just talked about it, and nothing happened. The situation reminded me of the Eugene O'Neill play *The Iceman Cometh*. The characters spend the entire play in a saloon talking about leaving, yet no one leaves. (Nick, one of my acquaintances, actually left Hewlett-Packard and started his own company. I was so delighted that I bought him a case of champagne. Now, forty years later, he is probably still wondering why I did it.)

This gave me the idea that students need to learn not to wait until after they graduate. Many students develop the idea that they're supposed to follow a prescribed path, in which they're not allowed to achieve anything until after they get a diploma. And if they don't develop the habit of doing things of their own volition, they will not change after they graduate. Many of the greatest entrepreneurs already had their businesses going during college—and many never graduated. Today's clearest example is Mark Zuckerberg and four fellow students, who started Facebook from the dorms at Harvard University.

Based on this thought, I decided the class project directive would be: Do something you have really wanted to do and have never done, or solve a problem in your life.

The projects served to introduce the achievement habit. Students learned they did not need to wait for some future time to take command of their lives. Doing this ten-week project of their own choice gave them a sense of empowerment that in many cases carried over into the rest of their lives.

You too can stop waiting for Godot and learn to do things that you have always wanted to do. If you start doing, and also apply the ideas in this book toward ridding yourself of unwanted issues, the chances are good that you too will have a much more interesting and fulfilling life.

Hugh Laurie, the doctor in the TV show *House*, said in an interview with *Time Out New York*, "It's a terrible thing, I think, in life to wait until you're ready. I have this feeling now that actually no one is ever ready to do anything. There's almost no such thing as ready. There's only now. And you may as well do it now. I mean, I say that confidently as if I'm about to go bungee jumping or something—I'm not. I'm not a crazed risk taker. But I do think that, generally speaking, now is as good a time as any."

IT'S LIKE RIDING A BIKE

A friend recently told me that she wanted to learn to ride a bike. She's a woman in her thirties, so I wondered why she had never learned as a child. What were the issues that had prevented her from learning thus far? My first assumption was that she must have lived in a busy city.

"No, the suburbs," she said. "I tried to learn, but I have a terrible sense of balance. I never got it."

It was a good time to check out problem solving through design thinking, so we went through the steps. First I had to make sure she was solving the right problem. Did she really want to learn to ride a bike, or was there a higher-level problem that she needed to solve? I asked her why she wanted to do this now.

"My daughter just learned how to ride a bike, and she's good at it. Right now, I can just jog alongside her and keep up, but I won't be able to do that for long. I want to learn so I can ride with her."

The problem one level up was that she wanted to be able to keep up with her daughter, and I had enough empathy to see it through her eyes. Working on bike riding seemed a good way to tackle it. So it was time to ideate: How could she learn to ride a bike?

"I figured I'd just go to a bike shop and ask them for the easiest bike to ride," she said. And that was one possible solution, however, what if she encountered the same balance problems she had as a child? She indicated that she still got dizzy easily.

We talked through a few ideas: She might take a yoga class to improve her balance. She might see a doctor to find out if she needed medication for an inner ear problem. She could take lessons, or she could put training wheels on an adult's bike. That one made her laugh, but fortunately it led to a more serious potential solution.

"You know, there are three-wheelers for adults," I said. A light bulb went off; she hadn't considered that. Sure, they might look a little odd compared to sleeker road bikes, but it would solve her problem instantly, without the need to really "learn" to ride a bike. She could keep up with her daughter (which was the higher-level problem) and skip right over the balance problem. It's just what a friend of mine had done when her aging body had given up on regular biking and her mind had not.

She felt so good about this solution that I did not bother exploring other ways for her to keep up with her bike-riding daughter.

This is the power of working with a partner or team: we each have different experiences and perspectives to lend. I was able to give her an instant solution to a problem she'd been putting off tackling because it seemed too difficult. It enabled her to stop thinking and start doing.

ACTING UNDER PRESSURE

Something we read in my class is "Tractoring Off," an excerpt from *The Grapes of Wrath* by John Steinbeck. It tells the story of a confrontation between a Dust Bowl farmer whose land has been foreclosed by the bank and a young tractor driver who is hired to plow the land, in the process destroying the farmer's house and farm. The tractor driver grew up in the neighborhood, and the farmer knows him and his father.

After the class has read the story, I ask for a show of hands as to how many people would choose to drive the tractor if they had no better means of supporting their family. Then I ask how many would not drive the tractor and how many aren't sure. I get about 45 percent on either side and about 10 percent undecided.

This essay represents a classic moral issue. The tractor driver realizes that what he is doing is destructive to the farmer and the farmer's family, yet he feels he has little alternative if he is going to support his own family. Ultimately he rationalizes his position by telling the farmer that if he does not do it, someone else is going to plow the land and destroy the farm. Even if the farmer shoots him, someone will come tomorrow and do the job. This rationalization and justification—"If I don't do it, someone else will"—is very common. So is the variant "I had to take care of my family," and the slightly less philosophical "I was just following orders."

I like this essay because it gives me a great opening to share with students my belief that they have no way of knowing what they will do when they are actually confronted with a comparable moral dilemma. I tell them that in moments of crisis in my own life, I have found that I did not always act in keeping with my self-image.

Once my wife, Ruth, and I were traveling around France by car. She was driving, and our younger son was in the backseat. We rounded a turn at the top of a hill and saw a line of cars stopped at a traffic light at the bottom. Ruth tried to slow the car down, and nothing happened. She shouted that the brakes were not working. After a moment of terror, I felt relaxed and comforted by the sense that at least all three of us would die together. Fortunately, the only one to die was the car, which was totaled; neither my family nor the unfortunate French family we plowed into was injured.

In fact, the French driver was very gracious. In spite of our having ruined the trailer that he was towing on the way to his family holiday, he suggested that because we could not do anything until the rental agency and the tow truck company reopened after their lunch break, we might as well all have lunch together. To my later embarrassment, I was much too upset to accept his generous act of civility.

Shortly after the crash, I figured out what had happened. The car had a manual transmission, and Ruth, who was used to driving an automatic transmission, had mistakenly put her foot on the clutch rather than the brake. I felt really stupid! Instead of blissing out over our impending deaths, I should have reached my foot over and stepped on the brake (or told her to do it), or pulled up the emergency brake, or jammed the car into reverse—anything other than what I did! I am usually so clearheaded and action-prone in emergencies. What happened to me? This was not the Bernie I know.

I had a similar experience when a good friend and colleague was being considered for a promotion. A question had arisen in the provost's office about his effectiveness as a classroom teacher. It fell to me to survey his current class. I was asked to have the students fill out rating forms. I did what I was asked and collected the completed forms. I looked over the forms in the privacy of my office and I realized that a few of them would cause difficulty. The promotion would not go through if I sent them on to the provost's office.

I hesitated. I knew my colleague was a good teacher, although his style was unorthodox, and not all students appreciated his creative approach. I also did not believe the survey forms were a good measure of his teaching. Most of all, I thought of myself as being loyal to my colleague and I certainly did not share many of the values the provost's staff used in judging people. With all these factors on the side of "losing" a few of the forms, my self-image at that time was that I would not turn them in. However, in the end I did forward the entire package.

I resolved my moral crisis by doing exactly what I was sure I would not do. Fortunately this was not a matter of life or death. My friend was unhappy for a time. However, his promotion was delayed for only one year, he went on to a distinguished career, and he has lived—more or less—happily ever after.

Although it can be interesting to read about another's situation and pass judgment about how you might have handled it differently, it's more useful to look at your own life. By examining your own rationalizations and moral compromises, you can better understand the complexity and unpredictability of peoples' ethical and moral decisions.

I faced a dilemma when Dave, the CEO of a company in Berkeley that designed custom automation equipment, invited me to lunch to talk about joining the company's board of directors. As we talked, some of the plans Dave had about the use of automation instead of actual humans in jobs pushed my buttons. It was a difficult spot: I didn't want to be associated with anything that would take away people's jobs, and yet I was tempted by the offer—which included substantial stock options. I was sure that if I told him about my objections, it would kill the deal.

It was a moment of pressure, and I needed to give him an answer. I told him that I would not accept his offer. He asked me to explain my decision. After I detailed my objections, he assured me he shared my concerns and would not be doing the things I objected to. Did I really believe it? I wasn't sure. Automation is designed to take away human tasks, after all . . . yet all it took was that little nudge to get me to set aside my conscience. I acquiesced and agreed to join the board.

My experience on the board was quite positive on both technical and personal levels. Several years later the company was sold to a large corporation, and my stocks brought me one of the largest single financial gains of my life. Looking back, I always remember how sure I was at that lunch that by voicing my objections I would kill the deal. What actually happened was quite the opposite.

I learned two big lessons that day. First, I believed I could know how someone else would react, but you can't. You can never be sure what someone else is thinking. Second, I was sure I would resist temptation, yet when push came to shove, I easily rationalized away my principles once someone gave me an excuse to do so. It gives me a lot of compassion for friends who, at the crucial moment, choose to drive the tractor.

A classic study of anxiety over how one will act under pressure is described in Stephen Crane's *Red Badge of Courage*. This novel gives us a vivid psychological portrayal of a young soldier beset by the anxiety that under fire he will be overcome by fear. As the war proceeds, he exposes his cowardice and ultimately his heroism. Like this young soldier, regardless of our self-image, it is difficult to know beforehand how we will actually act under pressure.

RESEARCH AND STATISTICS

When you make decisions based on "the research," you can easily be led astray by researchers' biases, which can lead them to make false claims and exaggerations.

I have spent most of my professional life publishing research papers, so I feel I know something about research. I understand scientific research processes and their limitations. Furthermore, as they say, some of my best friends are scientists. Some of them are even psychologists and behavioral scientists, and I have witnessed—and even been a subject in—a few of their experiments.

Based on all these experiences, I feel that in studying human behavior, it is really hard to come up with categorical statements. There is a lot of potential for misinterpretation, exaggeration, and just bad science. So I am often put off when someone uses such phrases as "Science shows," "The research shows," or "The fact is, there is science behind this." I wish that we *did* know all the things that are claimed. Although there is a lot of good—and even great—science, I do feel claims of scientific verification are at times exaggerated and unwarranted when it comes to human behavior.

The overreach of science probably arose because of the many unsubstantiated claims and ridiculous belief systems being bandied about. To combat this fraud, exploitation, and just plain ignorance, a sort of scientific vigilantism has developed. For some people, nothing can be considered valid without the imprimatur of science. My main concern is that when we insist on claims of scientific veracity, we downgrade or even rule out important sources of personal wisdom that exist independent of formal experimental verification.

Unfortunately, experimental verification is itself also a rather imperfect tool. I think it is important to understand that every time someone uses the word *science* or *research*, he is talking about the work not of some omnipotent beings with access to revealed truths but of fallible people working in a currently accepted paradigm and socialized into a scientific family and job structure. What it comes down to is that it is hard to convincingly prove or disprove things experimentally unless they already fit into people's belief systems.[1]

YOUR TURN

Do—don't *try*—this: list as many of your core beliefs as possible, and then ask yourself what basis you have for each belief. My own experience is that, unsurprisingly, a large number of my core beliefs come from my parents, the social and physical environment I grew up in, and my various peer groups. The next question to ask is, Which of your beliefs still serve you, and which have become dysfunctional and are best discarded?

Even when the data is sound—like the fact that half of all marriages end in divorce—does that mean that you should give up the idea of getting married because it has too high a potential failure rate? Statistics can show you trends, they can't predict your life.

Likewise, consider that the odds have *always* been against greatness. If one were to decide on a career path just by the odds of financial success, we would have no movie stars, authors, poets, or musicians. The odds of any one person becoming a professional, self-supporting musician are very low—and yet turn on the radio and you can hear hundreds of them. The odds were against the Beatles, Elvis, and the Grateful Dead, too. They could have been "scientific" about the whole thing and chosen more reasonable career paths, and what a loss for the world that would have been!

If you succeed, the odds are meaningless. Any path may have a 2 percent success rate, yet if you're in that 2 percent, there's a 100 percent chance of success for you. The long shots are often the most rewarding.

THE GIFT OF FAILURE

Oprah Winfrey was fired from her first job as a television anchor. That's a good thing; can you imagine what she would have missed out on if she'd gotten comfortable as a reporter in Baltimore? Dr. Seuss's first book was rejected by dozens of publishers and saw the light of day only because a friend agreed to publish it himself. Thomas Edison failed numerous times when trying to produce a light bulb, so many times that he famously said, "I have not failed. I've just found ten thousand ways that won't work."

Almost without exception, people who have done great things have also experienced great failures—and in many cases, getting fired or a similar devastating failure turned out to be a gift that allowed them to ultimately find great success.

As you now know, at the d.school, one of the basic principles is a *bias toward action*: that is, it is better to start to do something and fail than it is to do nothing and wait for the correct path of action to appear. Failure is part of the result to expect if you have a bias toward action.

The idea is not to be paralyzed in the face of uncertainty. If you do something and it works, great! If you do something and it fails, maybe even better. You do, you fail, and you learn. You do again, you fail again, and you learn some more. If you are mindful about what you have done, failure is a teacher. With a little luck, after enough failures you will succeed. In many cases this is a much better approach than a long, drawn-out investigation into the right way to proceed.

Nobody wants to fail, and yet we all do. Don't be afraid of failure. It is part of the price you pay for action; there's no need to sweep it under the rug and pretend it does not exist. The most liberating way to acknowledge failure is to celebrate it.

Let's look at circus clowns. When they unintentionally drop an item they are juggling, they often jump up with arms outstretched, a big smile, and a loud *ta-da!* My former colleague Rolf Faste used to have participants in our workshop take the clown's *ta-da* bow when they messed up. It did wonders; it made it okay to show one's mistakes and not try to cover them up. The accepting-repeated-failure route, if used with an open mind, can lead to much better solutions than does a fear of failure. A system that punishes failures rather than accepting that they occur on the road to success squelches creativity.

People tend to accept the notion that failure can be productive as an abstraction, yet unsurprisingly, in reality they find it difficult to accept failure unless they're in an environment that supports this notion. In the d.school we have had a great deal of success in creating such an environment. It is incredible to watch graduate students free themselves from the thrall of an entire career based on the principle that it is bad (or even catastrophic) to make a mistake. The pressure disappears, they feel reborn, and they often produce amazing results.

IT'S SUCCESS, STUPID!

My seventh- and eighth-grade years are blank in my memory save for the bottle cutter I built. That one experience stands out; I recall every detail of the project. I remember the fruit market where I found the crate to dismantle and use as a wooden base. I recall the purchase of a three-foot length of nichrome wire. This was the heart of the device. A thin wire made of nichrome has high electrical resistance and becomes red-hot when electricity passes through it, as it does in toasters and hair dryers. When wrapped around a glass bottle (no plastic in those days!) the red-hot wire gets the glass hot enough to crack if the bottle is plunged into cold water. If the wire is thin enough and the wrap is tight enough, you get a perfect break and the bottle splits into two perfect pieces, the neck and the base. I thought it was magical, although I have no recollection of needing to cut bottles for anything.

The only teacher I can recall is Mr. Dill, the science teacher who inspired the project and who feigned mild annoyance when I came to him after class for advice. I also vividly recall discovering the hard way that I needed to have my own fuse on the device if I did not want to blow the fuses in the entire apartment.

It was a memorable experience because it was the first time I can remember really making something on my own. I discovered I could make something real in the world. It was a formative experience that increased my self-esteem and gave me self-efficacy. Although I did not realize it at the time, that small success presaged a life of deriving great satisfaction from figuring out how to do things on my own and solving problems.

I've noticed that similar early experiences have stayed with many of my colleagues. David Kelley talks about how, when he was young, he succeeded in taking the family piano apart. My friend Vic talks more about his youthful science project than the sophisticated robot designs that subsequently made him famous.

Even habits such as reading are learned by building upon small successes. I recall how empowered I felt as a child after I read my first complete book. From that point on I was a reader. Later, as I got busy with my professional life, I lost the reading habit. So when I started to teach my "Designer in Society" course, I put readings into it—as much for my own sake as for that of the students. I ask them to read a book a week for eight weeks, and that regular activity gets all of us used to making time in our lives for reading. I have regained the habit, and many students tell me how thankful they are to have it as an unexpected side benefit of my course.

Success opens the door for increased self-esteem. If it comes early in life, it can do much to shape your future direction. If it does not come early, it can still be achieved. It is important to attempt different modalities and not to remain stuck in one that does not nurture and fulfill you.

Fear of failure often keeps us in an unsatisfying routine. Instead of daydreaming about change, reach out and attempt new things. Small steps with accompanying successes lead to major life transitions.

YOUR TURN

Did you have a youthful formative experience of accomplishing something on your own? Think back to the essence of that experience. Looking at your current life, what would you do differently if you were not afraid of failing or looking bad? In the next week, attempt something new in one of these areas. At first take a small step forward. Then, in each of the three subsequent weeks take an additional step. If you trip, pick yourself up and keep moving forward.

THE MAIN CONSTRUCTS OF this chapter are easy to test in your own life: Be honest and notice the differences between your self-image and the ways you actually act. Notice the difference between *intention* and *attention*, between *trying* to do something and actually *doing* it. Finally, notice how the habit of acting on your dreams builds from direct experience, and from overcoming the fear of failure.

WATCH your LANGUAGE

CHAPTER 6

Sincerity—if you can fake that, you've got it made.

—George Burns

The way we communicate with people has a significant effect on their opinions of us. It's not just about what we say, but about how we say it. Becoming better communicators can heal relationships, lead to better job opportunities, and enable us to reach wider audiences with whatever messages we want to share.

Language influences the way we see things. Public relations specialists and advertisers certainly know and exploit this, as do politicians, governments, and all sorts of spin artists. It has long been known that using different labels for the same thing will promote different behaviors. For our purposes it is important to understand what we do to ourselves with our own choice of words and use of language. Once we are aware of our usage, we can adjust our language to be more in keeping with our true intentions and the existential situations we are describing.

YES/NO

Let's start with a simple dichotomy: yes and no. There are situations in which we say one thing and mean the other. Some cultures, for example, recognize specific situations where it is considered impolite to say no; in others it is considered polite to say no when one means yes. For instance, in Iran, you're expected to refuse at first when a host offers you food or drink. Only after he pushes you to accept are you supposed to say yes.

I often use *yes* and *no* in a simple exercise. I pair people and ask them to have a conversation where one person repeatedly says yes, and each time, the other person answers with no. After some minutes I ask them to reverse roles: the yes person now becomes the no person, and the no person becomes the yes person.

Most people find it easier to say yes. A substantial number, however, report being more comfortable saying no, and very few report no difference. For me the interest is in the dynamic between the two people. It can take many forms. For example, it can have the form of an argument, a simple sober conversation, a big joke, or even a courtship. The point is for the participants to experience the big difference between the lyrics and the music in a conversation. In this exercise, I wrote the lyrics— *yes, no, yes, no, yes, no*—and the participants got to write the music and even the choreography (what tone and body language they used when they delivered their yes or no). After they think about this exercise, people often find something in their choice of music that helps them reach greater self-understanding.

AND/BUT

The lyrics tend to dominate the music for the words *and* and *but*. The existential situation almost always calls for the conjunction *and*, not *but*. Yet we often use *but* in place of *and*. This substitution is so common that it sounds correct. Unfortunately it often has the effect of changing a neutral statement into a negative one.

Let's take an example: "I want to go to the movies, *but* I have work to do." The sentence uses the conjunction *but* to tie together two phrases: "I want to go to the movies" and "I have work to do." Let's assume that the existential situation is that they are both true. Then, in fact, the actual situation is represented by "I want to go to the movies, *and* I have work to do." Existentially, movies and work are not in opposition. The word *but* is okay in common usage, *and* it does not reflect the true situation.

When you use the word *but*, you create a conflict (and sometimes a reason) for yourself that does not really exist. With the word *and*, there is no issue. You might or might not choose to go to the movies or to work. The use of *but* closes off the conversation space, while *and* opens it up. Furthermore, what follows the *but* is often bullshit reasoning. In improvisation terms, *but* is blocking; it is to be avoided as much as possible.

Where are you putting your *but*s?

Whatever you're trying to achieve, notice where you're blocking yourself by shutting down the conversation with a *but*. Let's say your goal is to get a popular internship, and it requires extensive travel. "I want this internship, *but* I'm afraid of flying," you tell yourself. What your brain then hears is, "Oh, well, *c'est la vie*. Guess we're not doing this internship."

When you open up the dialogue with "*and* I'm afraid of flying," your brain gets to consider how it can deal with both parts of the sentence. Maybe you'll see a therapist about it. Maybe you'll practice meditation.

The problem is that if you only use *and* in conversation,

you sound weird. I did an experiment years ago and went an entire weekend using *and* rather than *but*. Believe me, you don't want to do it.

I often handle the situation when I find it prudent to say *but* out loud by simultaneously converting it to *and* internally. This works well, except when someone who has taken a workshop from me hears the *but*, and shows how smart they are by publicly correcting me. I smile, *and* I hate it. Please don't be a smart-ass; just fix yourself. If you want to fix your friends and family, just give them a copy of this book. It will be much better for your relationships.

YOUR TURN

To get the flavor of this, the next five times you use the word *but*, simply change it to *and* in your mind. Do this silently by repeating to yourself what you just said out loud, with only this one word changed. Notice how it feels.

HAVE TO/WANT TO

Next on our list of words to be used as little as possible is the phrase *I have to*. The true situation is usually best described instead by *I want to*. Rather than argue with people about this, I always have them do a simple exercise, one that works best with a partner. You compose a sentence that starts "I have to." Your partner repeats the sentence with "You want to" substituted for "I have to." For example, you say, "I have to finish my work" and your partner replies, "You *want* to finish your work."

This works for just about anything, and can show you how much your own choice and desire play a role in decisions that you think are imposed on you. For example, "I have to breathe" turns into "I want to breathe."

"What? I do have to breathe!" you might say.

That's true . . . if you want to stay alive. You have the option to commit suicide and stop breathing. Choosing to continue to breathe is a good tactic if you want to stay alive.

YOUR TURN

To get the flavor of this, change *have* into *want* in your mind the next few times you say "I have to." Do this silently, simply repeating to yourself the sentence that you just said out loud, with just the one word changed.

This exercise is very effective in getting people to realize that what they do in their lives—even the things they find unpleasant—is in fact what they have chosen. Occasionally, someone gets stuck on an item or two. A good example of this is what happened with my good friend Ozgur. While he was a student in my course, he could not bring himself to say that he wanted to take the math courses that were a required part of his master's degree program. In fact, he knew he definitely did not want to take them, and certainly wouldn't take them if they were not required.

After graduation he went to work in industry for a year and then returned to Stanford to do his PhD. One of the first things he did upon his return was to seek me out and invite me for a Turkish dinner in San Francisco. He told me at dinner that even though he still found the master's degree math requirements odious, he realized he actually had wanted to take those courses, because the benefit to him considerably outweighed the discomfort. It was worth the wait for me: I love Turkish food, and that meal started a tradition in which, over the next few years, we sampled every Turkish restaurant in the area.

Even if Ozgur had not had the belated realization about the

math requirement, the have to/want to exercise would still have made its point for him. It is important to realize that everyday life is not an exact science. In some fields, such as mathematics, a single counterexample is sufficient to prove that something does not work. By contrast, my view of life is that if you do something and it works almost all of the time, then you might as well take it as a guideline.

If Ozgur had examined his entire life and the only thing he found that he had to do and did not want to do was the math requirement, then he might as well live his life as though he wanted to do everything he did. Have you ever heard the phrase "The exception proves the rule"? Well, if you have to struggle to find a single exception, you might as well live your life as though the rule is valid.[1]

CAN'T/WON'T

Next let's look at *I can't* and test it against *I won't*. A good way to make the test is to use the same procedure as in the previous exercise. So, for example, if you said out loud, "I can't stop breathing," you would then say to yourself, "I won't stop breathing." The simple change of *can't* to *won't* is often empowering. *Can't* implies helplessness; *won't* signifies volition and choice.

Similar word-change exercises worth doing are: *I need* changed to *I want* and *I'm afraid to* changed to *I'd like to*. Try these out the next time you notice yourself saying *I need* or *I'm afraid to*. These simple substitutions make a difference. They add empowerment to how you feel about yourself and your actions.

HELP AND SHOULD

Two other words that are good to discard or minimize the use of are *help* and *should*. If you think about *help* versus *assist*, the difficulty with the use of *help* becomes clear. When you *help* someone, you may be treating her as though she is helpless and only you are capable. By *assisting* someone you are treating her with dignity and saying that she, too, is capable. *Assisting* is empowering language; *helping* can at times be disempowering language.

Similarly, *should* is a disempowering word. It implies doing something under obligation—sort of a *have to* rather than a *want to*. The exercise that I like to do with this word entails having one member of a pair utter a sentence that starts with "I should . . ." The partner then responds, "What is a *should*?" After about two minutes of this nonsense, the *should* person gets the idea, and it is time to switch roles so that the partner can realize the absurdity of most *should*s. It is almost as much fun to do both sides of this exercise yourself.

WHY QUESTIONS

Avoid asking *why* questions when possible in interpersonal communications. When you ask someone why he did something, the word has a slightly negative, disapproving connotation, making him feel a need to defend himself.

Instead, state your position clearly, using *I* statements. Instead of asking, "Why did you choose Jane as your coleader?" say, "I felt hurt that you didn't choose me to colead."

Straightforward, honest conversation saves time and achieves your goal effectively. In this example, the answer to why Jane was chosen might be any *goooood* reason, and it most probably would not give you an opening to say that your feelings were hurt.

QUESTIONS IN GENERAL

Factual questions, questions of opinion, and rhetorical questions are the most common questions used in normal conversations.

It is important to realize that *not all questions are genuine ones.* Most people know there is no real question behind the customary greetings "How are you today?" "Are you having a good day?" and "How are you feeling?" People are not expecting a real answer.

These seemingly meaningless questions demonstrate goodwill and can be used to acknowledge another's humanity. When I'm asked these questions by strangers, I usually assume goodwill on their part and play the game by answering as expected. However, it is harder for me to behave when the other person is obviously preprogrammed as part of her job. On one occasion, the devil possessed me. I had the following conversation with a checkout clerk at a supermarket:

SHE: How are you today?
ME: I am dying of cancer.
SHE: That's good.
ME: Have a good day.

Clearly she did as expected, and did not care about or even listen to my answer.

In addition to using questions as greetings, some people regularly ask them simply to fill space. They feel they need to say something, so they ask a question. Like the checkout clerk, they don't really care about the answer; their attention goes elsewhere, and they don't actually even listen to it. Sometimes they deliver another question before the other person has finished answering. In these cases the specific question is clearly irrelevant. If the questioner does not care about the answer, it is not a *genuine* question.

In a teacher-student or boss-worker relationship, questions

can also be used as status symbols. If I'm the teacher and students ask me questions, then it shows that they respect me—they want to know my answers! They think I'm smart. Right?

Or it could really be the reverse: they want to be seen asking smart questions. Ever see someone blather on and on at a meeting, using big words, under the guise of asking the speaker questions, and suspect she just wants the people in the room to hear what she herself has to say? A person who is told "That's a good question!" gains status. Being seen engaging with a person of authority on a seemingly equal plane can be the whole goal.

One summer I taught a class for young researchers at a Bulgarian resort on the Black Sea. I was looking forward to the farewell party on the last evening after a long week. When I arrived at the party, it was already in full swing. I headed for the drinks table and poured myself a glass of wine. When I turned to face the room, everybody was sitting on the floor and looking at me. I asked the professor in charge what was happening. He told me they wanted to ask me questions.

Spending the evening answering questions was the last thing I had in mind, yet I did not want to be rude; I felt I had to be responsive. So I asked all who had questions to raise their hands. It looked like everybody had a question. For a moment I saw my hopes for a pleasant evening of debauchery fading away. Desperate, I asked that they all close their eyes and imagine they were talking to me, asking me their question. Then I asked them to imagine me answering their question. Finally I asked them to open their eyes and raise their hands if they did not get an answer. No one raised a hand. So I said, "Good. Everyone stand up, and let's party."

I am to this day convinced there were no genuine questions in that room—they had had all week to ask me whatever they wanted. I am especially pleased that I did not let whoever set up that question scenario hook my ego. Whatever answers they gave themselves did not get in the way of us all having a genuinely nice evening.

For it to be a *genuine* question, the questioner needs to be seeking information. For example, "What is your name?" "What time is it?" and "What's the quickest way to the airport?" all appear genuine. Yet we cannot be sure unless we find out whether the questioner really cares to know the information. "What is your name?" could just be a space-filling question. "What time is it?" could be flirtation. "What's the quickest way to the airport?" could be your coworker's way of trying to get you to ask about the exciting trip she's about to take.

Some questions are powerful in that they promote a transformative interaction. If when you ask about something, you intend to get yourself and others thinking about it, you are asking a *generative* question. If in addition you genuinely care about it, such questions are both *genuine* and *generative*; they promote a dialogue in which all parties are listening to others and are fully engaged. The questioner does not simply get back the "right answer." The question promotes a conversation between the answerer and the questioner that alternates between inquiry and advocacy. Truly generative questions are productive for all concerned. They result in much more than simply passing on known information.

Achieving is often tied to interpersonal relationships—in short, we're better together. When your coworkers and superiors respect you, you tend to go farther. When your friends feel you genuinely care, you form more lasting and meaningful friendships. Even on a subconscious level, people pick up on it when you're asking throwaway questions. Don't fill the space with them. If you're going to ask your coworker "How's your day?" be present for the answer.

CONTEXT

The context of your words has a big influence on how they are meant and how they are received. I have had the experience of saying something to someone and then being surprised when I learned that they had heard something completely different.

My wife and I were leaving a party at the Stanford Faculty Club. As we walked out the front door, Ruth said to me, "Boy, I am glad to get out of there."

Ron, my department chairperson and the host of the party, was directly behind us and overheard her remark. He said, "Ruth, it wasn't that bad, was it?" She then had to explain that her shoes were killing her and she could not wait to get to the car to take them off. She assured him that she had very much enjoyed the party. It was the truth. I am not sure to this day if Ron really believed her.

Although there are many causes for misunderstanding, one of the most important is the context in which the communication takes place. In teaching, the misalignment of context is one of the biggest causes for misunderstanding. Just as with Ruth and Ron, the student may be *talking* about her shoes while the teacher is *hearing* about the party. Clearly, the same words have totally different ideas behind them unless the context is shared.

In class I find that a good way to make sure we all share the same context is to have students ask questions about the course material. Periodically I require students to ask questions. If the class has twenty or fewer students, I require each one to ask a question. For larger classes, I just take a random sample. I am often blown away by how different some students' contexts are from what I had assumed. I'll have them ask any question, the dumber the better, and find out that some of them have been completely misinterpreting the lessons. This is a great tool for getting everyone into the same context before anyone gets too lost to recover.

I do a lot of work with colleagues from different disciplines and countries. There again contexts are critical for meaningful conversations. Many years ago I introduced a course titled "Computer-Aided Design." My close friend and colleague Doug wanted to sit in. We both have strong mathematics backgrounds: mine from researching mechanical systems, and his from researching chemical systems. We are both quite informal and open with each other. I do not think the students had ever before (or after) experienced one professor lecturing and the other sitting in the audience and periodically calling out "Bullshit!"

After class, we realized that we had not been in a shared context; the same words had very different meanings in our respective fields. Doug and I had a good time, and the show energized the students, so it all turned out well. If we had not had direct and open lines of communication, it could have been a disaster.

CONVERSATIONS

In verbal communication, both the lyrics and the music count, but people often do not give the music enough credit. Even something as simple as the yes/no exercise can trigger a whole range of different experiences. The exercise can be done in an angry way, a boring way, an exciting way, an amusing way, a teasing way, a bland way, a seductive way, a loving way. The moral is that *the music can be more important than the lyrics.*

It can also be the case that the lyrics do not really matter.

The lyrics in many pop songs, for example, are there to create a mood and to engage us; they are not meant to be taken literally. Similarly, complaining about our situation is a great way to attract people's attention and get them interested in us even if we do not really want their advice.

What happens if you complain or gripe to your friends and they give you some advice? Do you thank them and take their advice, or do you respond with "Yes, but . . ."? If you do the latter, then it is a fairly strong sign that you just want to be heard and aren't interested in solving the problem.

This works both ways. So if you *help* friends solve their problems by giving them advice, and they respond with "Yes, but . . . ," it is a good sign they do not want your help in solving their problems. They simply want to be heard. They want to vent and share. They want you to listen to their song. The proper response then is a sympathetic ear and your affirmation of their feelings and experience.

I am always amused by my wife's friends giving each other advice to take an antihistamine for coldlike symptoms. These are women who have raised children to adulthood and been through countless colds and other common illnesses. They just want to complain. They do not need or want their friends' medical advice; they want a little sympathy. Mainly, they need the connection with their friends, because their own grown kids don't talk to them anymore.

Then there are the different communication styles. One of our adult sons is usually not interested in the prolonged telephone chats his mother prefers. This caused hurt feelings at first. Now they have worked out a system. If he really does not want to chat, he tells her, "This is a business call." He is even allowed to change the designation midcall. It has gone a long way toward getting each of them comfortable with the other's different conversational needs.

You can learn to do this with colleagues as well. Rather than going on and on, make sure you give the other person an out. Say things like "I can just give you the summary if you're busy," or "Do you want to hear about this now?"

I have a close friend who loves to home in on one person. He will get deeply engrossed in conversation with someone next to him at a dinner party. Often the other people at the table feel ignored. Furthermore, his conversation consists mainly of him talking, often telling stories of his adventures. Some years ago we were at a large party, and I noticed he spent the entire evening talking to a woman I did not know. The next day he remarked that it was a very enjoyable party. I asked him about the woman he was talking with. *He knew virtually nothing about her*; he had spent the entire evening telling his own stories. The mystery woman was obviously a good and patient listener.

I know a married couple who love to share with their friends the details of every casual encounter they have. They call this *debriefing*, and it seems to give them great satisfaction. It enhances the original experience for them and assists them in reliving their adventures. It is also an important way for them to relate to others.

I, on the other hand, find that giving lots of details about my experiences is much less satisfying than just savoring them in my own mind or writing about them. So when someone asks me to debrief, I intentionally mishear their request as "Be brief." Of course, I too have a need to connect and share my humanity, however, with me it usually turns out that less is more.

Even people with very different styles can still communicate effectively. For example, my wife, our children, and I all have different communication styles. Yet we do make it work. If you do not have a lot of experience communicating with someone, it is difficult to always know the appropriate way to get your message across. Each new circumstance presents its own challenges. Here are some guidelines that I have found useful:

- First, speak from your own experience and feelings as much as possible. In that way you take direct responsibility for what you are saying, and that makes it hard for others not to follow your lead and take responsibility for what they are saying. In judging others, you need to realize that you are simply giving your opinion. It is best to always speak from how it makes you feel or what you personally believe. Do not generalize or universalize your personal judgments. Make *I* statements.

- One of the most difficult things is to listen to someone else's story and not interrupt. Many people interrupt because they have something that they are afraid they might forget or that will not be relevant later. The best thing to do is to let it go. If it is still appropriate at the end, say it then. If it gets lost and remains unspoken—no matter how brilliant it would have been—the world will not notice!

- The next most difficult thing when you are a listener is not to follow immediately with one of your own stories. It may not be as relevant to the topic as you think, in which case the person who told the original story will feel you did not really listen or get the point of her story. Alternatively, if your story is on point and a better story, it will seem that you are playing at one-upmanship. The other person's story loses relevance, and she feels diminished—not supported—by your story.

I have a good friend who, after many years of marriage, went through a divorce. As soon as he separated from his wife, he went around to his close friends to inform them individually. Universally his announcement was followed by the listeners' tales of past crises in their own marriages. Understandably, his friends—me included—were trying to make him feel that we understood. Actually, he felt he wasn't being listened to. In retrospect, I realize I would have been a much better friend if I put aside my discomfort and talked to him about his feelings, not my stories.

The question of intention lies behind all communication. What is it that you intend to communicate? Simply saying something does not mean it has been actually communicated. I realized this very early on as a teacher. I would say something several different times, intending to make it clear that I was placing strong emphasis on it. Inevitably, if I asked an examination question about the item, I would get students saying, "It was unfair because you hardly touched on it in the lectures." This brought home the insight that the teachers' worlds and the students' worlds are very different, and that I have to take responsibility to make sure my communications have been received as intended.

Even if all parties agree on what has been said, or even if there is a signed, written agreement, it does not mean that everyone is really agreeing to the same thing. There are often honest misunderstandings.

These take place largely because people do not make sure their meanings—not only their words—are shared. Remember, successful communication takes both *intention* and *attention*. It requires the explicit intention that the meaning be shared, and it also takes the explicit attention to be sure it has been shared. Unless you have a strong experiential bond with someone, simply saying something is often not sufficient to really communicate it. Actors know that they cannot play a character well unless they know how that character thinks.[2] Similarly, true communication is facilitated when all the parties know how the others think.

Here are my top suggestions for good interpersonal communications:

1. Speak for yourself. Say "I know," "I think," "I feel," "My reaction is," not "Everyone knows," "We all think," "We all feel," "Everyone's reaction was." It is much better to take responsibility for what you say than to attribute it to others. You hardly know what you yourself really think, let alone what others think.

2. Don't be judgmental. If you need to be judgmental, especially in an argument or a tense situation, speak for your own feelings and reactions (as in item 1).

3. Acknowledge other people's issues. People want to know that you heard them. Acknowledge their problems only; don't try to solve them unless they explicitly ask you to. They don't want your advice or to know about your similar experiences; they just want to know that you have heard their story. It's about them, not you!

4. Don't ask *why* questions. Make declarative statements about your position. Asking people why they do things puts them on the defensive.

5. Really listen. Even if you think you know what they will be saying or you have heard it before, don't interrupt or tune out. Don't be in your head preparing your reply while they are talking. Be willing to lose your thought no matter how brilliant it is.

6. When you are telling a story, be clear what your point is. Be prepared to be misunderstood and misinterpreted. If it really, really matters, make sure your message got across by having it replayed to you.

7. Make sure your communication is heard as intended. Go beyond just delivering the message. Have the intention and attention to get it heard the way you mean it to be heard.

8. Make sure you understand what is being communicated to you.

Go beyond just good listening. Get to a point where you know the intention, not just the words. If you have any doubt, rephrase and repeat back what the person has just said: "So, what I'm hearing is . . . ," or "It sounds like you feel . . ." Try to get to the core of what a person is asking for or feeling, and then check to make sure you have it right. This is also known as "active listening," a phrase coined by

Thomas Gordon.[3] It may feel phony the first few times you do this (frequently rephrasing and repeating what another person says is not what most of us do normally), yet it can be very powerful. When another person feels understood, you've given him a great gift.

THE HARD CONVERSATIONS

Part of working well in any group is the ability to have hard conversations. It is easy to avoid having conversations that deeply go into your feelings and tough issues. Ironically, avoiding hard conversations usually makes things worse, not better. Properly conducted, hard conversations vastly improve matters and can totally change the atmosphere in a positive way.

I have found this to be the case both at work and at home. If one person takes the initiative, others usually follow. It is easy. All you have to do is say how you feel and what your concerns are, and make sure you aren't attacking the person.

I still recall the feelings of excitement and positive group cohesion thirty years ago when, at a faculty meeting, the Design Division got up the nerve to tell our youngest faculty member that we wanted him to leave. It was clear he would never complete his PhD thesis if he continued working at Stanford as a lecturer.

Everyone, including the person we were dismissing, spoke openly and from the heart. I have found over and over again that if one person speaks from his heart, others follow, and the group's feelings of community and commitment increase tremendously. On the other hand, if the discussions remain on a superficial and impersonal level, the feelings of frustration and alienation abound.

Sociologists speak of *realistic* and *nonrealistic* conflicts. A realistic conflict is a disagreement that is goal oriented. That is to say, it is about something specific that the conflicting parties need to resolve. When such conflicts arise in well-functioning relationships, their resolution can lead to progress toward the goal.

A nonrealistic conflict is, at heart, about something other than what is being talked about. Its primary purpose, for at least one of the participants, is to discharge tension. It is not really about the goal of solving a problem. Such conflicts arise when there isn't real mutuality in the group. Instead there is a *pseudomutuality* wherein people pretend their relationship to the others is something that it isn't.

They may be hiding a poor self-image or a sense of exclusion or jealousy. Whatever its root causes, they are suffering discomfort that builds up tensions. In provoking a nonrealistic conflict, they are seeking a temporary discharge of their built-up tensions. Unless something is done about the root causes of the tension, such conflicts can only put a temporary Band-Aid on a bad situation.

GOOD COMMUNICATION SKILLS AFFECT every area of your life. They can mean the difference between getting a job and not getting it, making an important connection with someone or not, and surviving public crises without too much damage to your reputation or becoming persona non grata. We elect presidents based more on their communication style than anything else. We value people who communicate openly and honestly, and we avoid people who don't pick up on social cues that we don't *want* to be cornered or kept on the phone for a half hour. The best communicator isn't necessarily the person who knows the fanciest words; it's the person who pays attention and makes others know that they've been heard.

GROUP HABITS

CHAPTER 7

Conversation while being driven in New York City
by my friend Harold:
Me: Harold, why don't you use your turn signals?
Harold: I don't like strangers to know my business!

Belonging to groups gives us an important way to express our humanity. Most of us are affiliated with many groups: In addition to family, we have groups of friends; professional, political, health, and school groups; and so on. The way you interact within those groups can change the way you feel about each situation and can enrich (or screw up) your life.

In this chapter we'll talk about making productive changes in your teamwork, physical space, body language, and communication to make groups work better for you.

WORKING IN TEAMS

In my teaching and administrative roles as the academic director of the d.school, most of my day is filled with different group experiences. In the d.school, all classes must be team-taught. The way we do team-teaching is different from many other team-taught courses at Stanford: we expect that the entire teaching team be present at every class, and always be ready to participate. Although there have been some remarkable exceptions, most other entities at Stanford treat team-teaching as a relay race: each person does his run, then hands off the baton to the next person, leaving the race.

We feel that if every member of the teaching team is participating, the students get a richer experience. My colleague Jim Adams loves this kind of teaching. He tells me, "I like to team-teach so we teachers can trash-talk each other, thereby giving the students a better insight into professors as people and the nature of their world." Unfortunately, most of my colleagues are not at Jim's level of enlightenment regarding the virtues of trash talk. Still, it does benefit everyone to have different viewpoints in the same room.

An iconic example of the benefits of team-teaching occurred when I received a phone call from Bill on the evening of our first class session. He and I were part of the teaching team for the class "Transformative Design." I was thrilled to be working with Bill because he was one of my closest friends, a world-class designer who had designed the first laptop computer, and one of the three people who had founded the design consultancy IDEO. The phone conversation went as follows:

BILL: I was wondering what you thought about our class this afternoon.
ME: I thought it was great. What did you think?
BILL: Yes, I liked it.
ME: Great!
BILL: Do me a favor. Next time, give me your PowerPoint slides the evening before the class.

ME: You already know what I am going to say. Why do
   you need them?
BILL: It's not the content. I want to fix your fonts.
ME: Are you kidding?
BILL: No.

Two evenings later Bill and his wife, Karin, were at my house
for dinner. I showed my PowerPoint slides to our wives—they
are both designers and have great aesthetic sensibilities. They
humored me by agreeing that my fonts were not bad. However,
I knew Bill was right: I had sinned in multiple ways. He pro-
ceeded to point out the defects: too many font styles, too many
different font sizes, no consistency of style, and—worst of all—I
had not used the official d.school font. As soon as he finished,
Karin dubbed Bill the Font Nazi. We all had a good laugh.

The next week I, of course, told the story to the class. That
incident provided me with a mantra for the rest of the term:
"Fix up your fonts, or Bill will get on your case." It was all in
good fun.

A powerful lesson lies behind this incident, however. I was
trained as an engineer; I am used to worrying primarily about
the content. Bill was trained as a designer; bad aesthetics made
him viscerally upset. If I were teaching the class alone, the students would never have been exposed to the sensibility that Bill
brought with him so naturally. The sharing of sensibilities and
different points of view enrich the educational experience for
students and for teachers, and this occurs when we bring teachers from different backgrounds into the same classroom.

Needless to say, Bill prepared all the future PowerPoint
slides, handouts, and Web postings for the class. Everything
was elegantly done in the same style, using the official d.school

font. I never fully recovered. Every time I look at fonts, I fondly remember Bill. I also curse him for all the extra time and effort I now put in struggling to get my presentations close to his minimal level of acceptance.

STUDENT TEAMS

We also require teamwork from the students. Most of our courses are based on project work from interdisciplinary student teams. We generally do not impose any structure on the ways student teams organize themselves.

Again, this is different from the mainstream. Many other academic units dictate team structure and assign different responsibilities to the students within the team. Much of the faculty mentality that team members should be assigned specific roles seems to me to be analogous to what happened to me in the third grade when the teacher assigned a structure, thinking it would train us for the real world. In fact, it had the effect of deadening initiative, discouraging us from learning the skills we needed to be responsible and flexible enough to find the appropriate structure for each specific situation.

Sharing a project requires a set of skills that are different from those used when working alone. Everything discussed in the "Conversations" section of chapter 6 is applicable to teamwork.

In addition, there is the added dynamic of multiple players. Generally the students are organized into groups of about four, so it is possible for there to be various splits in the way students handle conflict. We sometimes get three against one (or one against three!). We sometimes get two pairs, and sometimes one pair and two singles or, in the worst case, four singles. Remarkably, most teams work out well, and conflicts usually get resolved in productive ways. We actually have a professional psychologist on staff (we call him the d.shrink), and he promotes the idea that open communication leads to much better team performance.

There are various theories on how to compose teams to match different personality and skill types.[1] I find that the most important thing to be learned from studying about different personality types is the visceral acceptance of the fact that basic differences exist between people. People are different because they have different academic majors and because they also have different styles for learning and doing things. Each person needs to know that his way is not necessarily the only right way. This will serve him both on the job and in the family.

You know by now how much I like jokes, right? Well . . .

During a court case, after listening to the plaintiff, the judge says, "You're right."

The defendant gets excited and says to the judge, "But, Your Honor, what really happened was . . ."

The judge then says to the defendant, "You're right."

Hearing this, a spectator in the courtroom says, "Wait a minute, Your Honor; they can't both be right."

The judge responds, saying, "You're right."

The point here is that seemingly contradictory things can all be correct. Most real-world activities are not zero-sum games. Ways can be found in which everyone, and especially the team, moves forward. If it is done out of respect and caring, controversy is not a bad thing. It can even be a good thing. It is important that the controversy not get personal and damage the team's sense of mutual support and understanding.

It is also important that everyone on the team have an intention to make things work. Things go awry when people have different levels of commitment and different goals for the team. When things do not go well, it is easy for some team members to become self-righteous. It is good to know the truth, and it is good to know that the truth in itself does not dictate any specific action. As was pointed out in chapter 1, you give everything its meaning. So lighten up and assist the team to get the job done!

CONSTRUCTIVE CRITICISM

In our workshops we have adopted a system for criticism that I originally learned from the late George M. Prince in a Synectics workshop.[2] The idea is to give criticism in a supportive way that promotes positive evolution of the students' work, by saying two *I like* statements followed by one *I wish* statement. For example, I might say, "I like the way you took into account concerns about safety, and I like the way it looks." Then, after a short pause, I would continue, "I wish we could find a way to make it smaller."

The first thing to notice about this feedback is that there is no *but* between the *I like* and the *I wish*. They are separated by only a short pause, nothing else. The second thing to notice is that *I wish* is said in a way that encourages further refinement in a positive way. It enlists everyone who hears the comment, including the commentator, to work on figuring out a solution. The way *not* to say it would be "It will not work; you made it too big." This is a blocking kind of statement, whereas the *I wish* version says "Yes, *and*."

This system for criticism of student work was used for many years in our product design program. Now it has become a fixture in the d.school, where it is used for feedback to and from students. This type of evaluation is, in theory, done after each class session by the teaching team and by any students who wish to participate. In addition, sessions involving the entire class and teaching team are done during class every few weeks. Based on this, changes are made both to subsequent classes and future course offerings.

The current version of the *I like/I wish* system does not limit the order or number of these statements. Sometimes, a group does all the *I like*s first, followed by all the *I wish*es. A modified version has been introduced by people who do not follow the original idea behind the *I wish*. They use the *I wish* simply to state something they would like to change, without suggesting a direction for improvement. Then they add a third set of items given in the form of *what if?* These serve the function of the problem-solving aspect of the original use of *I wish*. Under this newer version we might get feedback such as, "I liked meeting as a group" or "I wish we spent more time in our group," and then "What if we met after class?"

Personally I am more comfortable with the original *I like/I wish* version when it comes to criticizing students' work. The *I wish* version works well when it is used to suggest areas for improvement. It has a positive pull similar to the question "How might we . . . ?" Both "I wish there was a way to accomplish _____" and "How might we accomplish _____?" are good ways to get people to move forward in a proactive problem-solving frame of mind.

Regardless of the version used, this feedback mechanism is effective. It is invaluable in the d.school's quest for continual improvement in teaching. The students and teaching team like it, and it adds a feeling of community to the class. The same tool can be profitably used for constructive criticism in many situations; it is certainly not limited to student work or to academia.

It can be usefully applied to both your personal and your professional lives.

We once had a senior member of the teaching team who had never before taught at the d.school and was used to the formal European academic tradition. At the end of the first class session, one of the Stanford professors explained to him that it was our custom to gather for an *I like/I wish* feedback session, and he agreed to join. However, when he realized that the session would also include students, he was taken aback. The idea of students telling him what they did not like seemed audacious to him. Still, he was a good sport and toughed it out. After a few such sessions, he became such a big enthusiast that when a class ran a little long and the other teaching team members wanted to forgo the feedback session, he was the one who insisted they follow through with it.

STYLES AND CULTURES

My wife Ruth's book club agreed to read an early version of the manuscript for this book. One of the members, Marcia, sent me an e-mail thanking me and telling me she liked what she had read. However, the Your Turn exercises scared her. That surprised me.

"What about shy people?" she asked.

That struck a note in me. It also brought back a terrible memory I had suppressed—probably my worst teaching error.

I was teaching a graduate class on designing mechanical devices. That day we were covering a set of parts called a four-bar mechanism. I had assigned students to find mechanical devices in their environments and to take turns in front of the class presenting an analysis relating what they found to what we were studying. The presentations went along well until one student did her presentation without regard to the vocabulary we had been using in class. I pointed at her projected diagram, showing a four-bar mechanism operating the tail flap on an airplane, and asked her what that was called. She did not answer.

I got angry and blurted out, "This is the fifth week of class. It is inconceivable to me that you would not be able to identify a four-bar mechanism. We have been talking about them twice weekly since the first class. Where have you been?"

The woman did not say a word. She left in tears and never returned. She was from China, and it was especially humiliating to her that I had caused her to lose face in front of the entire class. As soon as I realized what I had done, I felt terrible. Week after week I hoped she would return. To this day I regret that I did not reach out and contact her.

Two years later, she showed up in a class I was coteaching with Sheri Sheppard, designed to be supportive of women graduate students. Sheri was the only female professor in Stanford's Department of Mechanical Engineering at that time. We used some of the techniques presented in this book, and the class passed without incident. I noticed for the first time, however, how very shy this student was. I finally realized what a frightening experience being in front of the design class must have been.

At the final feedback session this student told me, "You were much nicer in this class than the last one." It relieved a bit of the guilt I carried for my previous insensitivity to her shyness.

We have many foreign students at Stanford. Some come from cultures that are fairly aggressive, and they tend to fit right in. Many others come from cultures where students are taught to be passive receivers of knowledge and to consider faculty as unapproachable, almost as deities. For such students, and for naturally shy American students, the Silicon Valley culture can be especially trying. Behaviors such as self-promotion, group work, approaching strangers, seeking assistance, meeting with an instructor during office hours, and speaking up in class can be difficult for them.

Nowadays, with people working, studying, and living in countries that were foreign to their forebears, analogous cultural difficulties exist in many parts of the world. This situation is especially worthy of attention when you have people from another culture who were born in your country or who speak your language. You must not assume that just because someone speaks your language well, she is comfortable with your culture. In interacting with others it is important to look for the outliers and take into account their discomfort with what may seem very natural to you.

Outliers can occur at both ends of the spectrum. I had a PhD student from Shanghai who was most unusual. In those days, before the economic upswing, most students from the People's Republic of China were supported by their government and lived frugally, worked diligently, and used bicycles or walked. They saved what money they could get to buy things to take back home. This young man did not fit the mold. He bought a car during his first few months. Then he started not showing up for our weekly meeting. When he did appear, I was not impressed by his output.

I gave this student several minor reprimands, yet his behavior remained spotty. Finally I'd had enough. Even though a close colleague in Shanghai had recommended him to me, it was time to end the relationship. I told him that I did not want to continue to work with him, and he should find another thesis advisor. He astounded me by telling me it was not fair to dismiss him in this manner. I asked him what he thought would be fair.

He suggested a point system similar to that used by the Department of Motor Vehicles: each offense has a specific number of points associated with it, and you lose your license only if your total exceeds a certain number of points.

This was too amusing to turn down. We agreed on a system of points. Amazingly, he shaped up immediately after our agreement, and never got close to having his "license" suspended. He finished in a reasonable time with a good thesis. After graduation he found a job on the East Coast, got married, had a child, and never went home to China.

On the other end of this spectrum, I find that when I go abroad, I am often the outlier. It takes a little courage to introduce a bit of interactive California teaching style. Once I was with a classroom of students in a regional college near Mumbai. After I worked hard to break the ice for about forty minutes, I got the students to open up and we had a nice interaction going. The director walked in and, after a few minutes of observation, decided he would "help" me. He loudly announced, "I request you do not interrupt the professor until after the lecture."

If looks could kill!

In any group setting it's important to realize that not everyone thinks like you do, whether because of cultural differences or just differences in style. Aim to understand each other's communication preferences and learn from each other.

WHEN WAS THE LAST TIME YOU . . . ?

I have often had the experience that after students miss a class, they come to me for the lecture notes. My style is to lecture extemporaneously, so I do not really have a set of lecture notes to give the student. Instead, I've proposed what seems to me to be a perfectly reasonable alternative. I suggest that the students copy a classmate's notes, go over them, and then come to me to discuss anything they feel unclear about. Often it turns out that the students don't know anyone else in the class, and they're not sure who to ask about borrowing notes. It's as though students in the same class are ships in the night, passing each other with just enough recognition to avoid collision.

My urge to assist students in breaking through this veil of anonymity was one of the factors that led me to create courses in which students interact with each other. In this context I devised an exercise that has been very effective in getting people to connect. This connection helps to break through the ships-in-the-night phenomenon of people being in the same environment and not connecting. Airplane travel has evolved into a classic example of people spending hours together, including sleeping next to one another, without communicating.

An effective group icebreaker is to divide the class into pairs in which each tells the other what type of person she is; this provides good experience in both talking and listening. The students then are asked to relate what they heard about their partner to a different group of partners. This is a good way for us to discover how poorly we listen and how little we remember.

After the first introductions, a great way to connect with a larger group is to form circles of six to eight people and have them each take turns completing the same sentence. The sentences I use always begin with "The last time I . . ." After everyone has completed his response to a given sentence, I introduce the next sentence to the group. This time a different person goes first, and when this round is completed, a new person begins with the next sentence. I use a different human experience for each round. They thus end up completing sentences such as:

The last time I laughed was . . .

The last time I cried was . . .

The last time I had trouble sleeping was . . .

The last time I did a good deed was . . .

The last time I got angry was . . .

The last time I did something brilliant was . . .

The last time I did something stupid was . . .

The last time I had a mystical experience was . . .

The last time I stole something was . . .

The last time I lied was . . .

The last time I thought about suicide was . . .

The last time I felt love was . . .

I have found this technique also works well with groups in settings outside the university.

This is a very effective exercise on several levels. It gets people to find out a little bit about each other and to start to form connections with others in the group. It is also a way for people to see that we all share a common basis of experience. We all laugh, cry, lose sleep at night, and do things we are proud of, things we are not proud of, things we regret, and things we are ashamed of. That is all part of the human experience.

We often hide parts of ourselves because we feel others would not understand or would disapprove; we are sure they do not do similar things. My experience is that students from all over the world have had similar emotional experiences—after all, we are all human. It goes a long way toward establishing trust when students tell their stories to each other. I arrange the room so that I do not hear the stories that go with the responses. I do this to emphasize that this is a student-to-student sharing experience.

It always turns out that the more you reveal about yourself, the more people like you. It is ironic that we hide aspects of ourselves because we fear rejection. It is the hiding, not the revealing, that leads to rejection.

YOUR TURN

Apply these same ideas in a private conversation. Next time you are having a leisurely conversation, tell your acquaintance what type of person you think you are and then ask her to tell you about herself. Then go on to share the last time you could not sleep all night and ask your partner when that happened to her. From there start trading stories about the last time you had a good laugh, the last time you made a bad mistake, and so on. At the end notice how your relationship with the other person has been altered by the details you shared.

THE NAME GAME

Some people identify strongly with their names, others hate their names, and many others are more or less neutral in their feelings. I have asked students to rate their feelings about their names on a scale from 1 to 10. I've gotten ratings all along the scale.

I used to do a class exercise in which I asked the students to shut their eyes and think about the name that best describes who they are, or if they feel they already have the correct name, to pick another one that just feels good. Then I asked them to mill around and interact with each other, staying in the persona that their new name implies to them. This is an interesting way to briefly try out "changing your skin."

If you are not happy with your given name, it is relatively easy to do something about it, either legally or simply by choosing to go by a name other than what's on your official documents.

Some people purposefully distort the pronunciation of their names to hide or downplay their ethnic origins, while others insist on an authentic ethnic pronunciation that seems exaggerated to outsiders. Choosing a less ethnic name is most commonly seen in show business. However, it also happens in the general workforce. A man named José Zamora reported that he was sending out hundreds of résumés and getting no responses until he removed one letter from his name and became Joe. It's terribly unfair, yet experiments have consistently proven that applicants with Latino names and "black-sounding" names (such as Lakisha Washington or Jamal Jones) don't get called for interviews nearly as much as those with "white-sounding" names (such as Emily Walsh or Brendan Baker).

People's relationships to their names are complicated. It is best not to assume anything. One thing is for sure: if you use someone's name, you take the relationship to a different level than when you do not. Many people mistakenly believe they have trouble remembering names. I have always found there is a lack of intention and attention underneath their defeatist attitude.

People take the time in some groups to have each person say her name aloud. This method seldom gets the names learned, and it is more a pretense than an actual taking of responsibility for the name issue. Name tags are a common tool for avoiding the issue of really dealing with names. It is easy with name tags to pretend that people know each other's names.

If we really want to handle learning people's names in groups, there are many ways to proceed. One is to break into subgroups of two people and then build up from there. The trick is to get something memorable from each partner. An easy way to do this is to come up with something unusual that you both share; this serves as a "hook." For anything—including a name—to be remembered, it must be dwelled upon and repeated. Thus, when you and your partner join another pair, you should introduce each other to the new pair and give them the hook that you both share. You can keep enlarging the group size and get everyone to repeat each person's name and the hook that goes with the name.

For groups of thirty or less I prefer to deal directly with the entire group, having everyone stand in a circle, and each person say his or her name in turn. In the low-stress version, the students repeat in unison the name they just heard. In the high-stress version, each person takes a turn and gives his name and the names of all the people who have gone before him. The exercise can, in both cases, become more fun, and the names get easier to remember (they become "stickier") if, in addition to his name, the student also simultaneously introduces himself with a whole-body physical gesture; then the others repeat both the name and the gesture. The gesture is easy to remember, and it makes the name easier to remember.

It is useful to reinforce this learning by giving each person a list of the names to take home, and, if possible, also photos. For subsequent group meetings I have photos and names posted in the room for easy reference.

Regardless of what we do in the group, I always assign myself the homework of learning names as soon as practicable—usually by the second meeting. Many teachers never learn their students' names. I never used to. Why bother? Now I realize that I just didn't want to devote any effort to it. I thought that if it didn't happen automatically, it was because I didn't have the ability. In reality, it has nothing to do with ability; it is a classic case of not giving the required attention to carrying out the intention. This is a sure way to develop a nonachievement habit.

People who perform prodigious feats of memorizing go through all sorts of special efforts to pay attention to what they are memorizing. They know you cannot memorize something without giving it particular attention. It is mindfulness rather than brain structure that differentiates "them" from "us."

On the other hand, you can assist others to remember your name. If you add a memorable hook when you introduce yourself, your name becomes easier to remember. People with difficult names also help others greatly by spelling their names. Even simple names can often be confusing. When I say my last name, people sometimes hear *Ross* rather than *Roth*. So I always spell it when I say it to strangers or over the phone.

Using names transforms relationships. I should have learned this years ago from my wife's college biology teacher, who memorized all the students' names before the first day of class. My wife immediately fell in love with him, as did many of his other students. To this day, fifty-nine years later, she still carries a crush.

Knowing names connects people at a much more satisfying level.

WHO'S IN CHARGE?

When people work in groups, the question of leadership arises. The issue of who leads and how the group is led can be spoken or unspoken, formal or informal. Much has been written about leadership and leadership styles. Growing up in America, I was brainwashed to believe that every organization needs a formal structure with a leader on top.

When I was in the third grade, the first thing we did when the teacher had us form a group was to elect a president, vice president, secretary, and treasurer. It was my teacher's way of preparing us for good citizenship. Nobody seemed to notice that the structure was functionally meaningless.

In the sixth grade we elected a mayor of our school. My friend Seymour was elected mayor of Public School 96 in the Bronx, and because I had mimeographed his election posters, he appointed me police commissioner. I guess it was good training for the real world, because I do remember using my high office to cover up my crimes (such as tardiness and truancy). In retrospect, these two experiences did more to brainwash me into believing we all need to work in a hierarchy than they did to make me into a contributing self-actualized citizen.

My experience at Stanford—regarding leadership, working with groups of colleagues and with groups of students—has been remarkable, and somewhat atypical. Originally I was a member of the mechanical engineering department, which had about twenty-five faculty members grouped into three divisions.

I was a member of the Design Division. The chairman chose a director for each of the three divisions; this was an efficient arrangement because he only had to deal with three professors, instead of all twenty-five. Most of the faculty members were content because someone else was doing their division's administrative work and they could devote their time to their own research and teaching. However, I started to notice defects in the organizational structure as my career developed.

The chairman could easily influence the division directors' behavior because he had a lot of control over the assets he allocated to them. If they were young, he also had a lot of control over their future careers. When tough issues came up, I felt the division directors were at times in a position where their own personal interests opposed those of the individuals they were representing. Furthermore, the directors were often not capable of truly representing the other members of their division. In the Design Division the situation came to a head when the director at that time took a leave, and he and the department chairman, without consulting the faculty in the division, attempted to install an unsuitable replacement.

It was the mid-1970s, and people were reconsidering many things within the social order. It was a time of student unrest, social protest, and the questioning of traditional societal structures and values.

At that time the Design Division had eight faculty members, and we unanimously decided to restructure our group to operate as a flat organization *without* a director. The department chairman raised many objections to our new structure. In rebutting the objections, I came to fully realize what a potentially powerful new form we had created. We had a good idea: that structure has been thriving for forty years, and the Design Division is now much more successful than it ever was.[3]

Our new structure hinged on an hour-long weekly meeting, open to all Design Division faculty and staff. The meeting had no chairperson; we simply went around the table, taking turns bringing up any issues that required the division's decision, reporting on past happenings, and announcing future events. We operated by consensus and negotiation, almost never voting on anything. There was almost no acrimony, and people treated each other with respect, collegiality, and a spirit of shared purpose and commitment.

We'd rarely had meetings with each other before this reorganization. Nobody but the director knew what was going on, and people took little or no responsibility for the "commons." Under the new system, there was a major transformation, and it was very exciting. We were all in charge, and we all wanted to make it work.

When we started, the department chairman's main objections were based on the idea that there would not be one director to represent the division's interests to the chair, and that we would be unmanageable. It turned out to be just the opposite. We now had the most powerful form of organization in the department because we were a large group of people with one voice.

It was impossible for the chairman or the dean to buy one person off. There were now eight faculty members behind each issue. If one of us had trouble getting promoted, a salary issue, or anything else that required support, we could send eight people—or any subset—to meet with the chairman or the dean. It was a powerful new model that allowed for the traditional single-director structure as one of its forms. If needed, we could appoint someone "director for a day"—we never actually did that.

We chose to divide up the jobs and rotate among them in order to be efficient and to make it easy for others to deal with us. One of us was responsible for the finances, another handled course scheduling, another represented us at the chairman's weekly meeting with the other divisions' directors; yet another person dealt with staff issues, and the dreariest position of all went to the person who dealt with office and classroom space. (To compensate, we decided to let him have the exalted title of Space Czar.)

All these jobs were regularly rotated, and new positions were created on an as-needed basis. We all had an equal voice. Those who cared most about an issue took on the leadership to get it handled. If nobody cared, we did not do much about that issue until someone wanted it resolved.

The new system went a long way toward creating a unique

and strong culture. Interestingly, whenever we acquired new faculty, by virtue of expansion or to replace people who retired or left for other reasons, they quickly adapted to become fully contributing members to this unique group. We have made some slight modifications to our meetings over the years; we now have a student representative at each meeting, and the non-teaching staff attend every other meeting. We have also added a second hour to allow for philosophical discussions.

I have developed a lot of respect for the power of flat organizations by virtue of my forty years of experience in the high-functioning Design Division. Furthermore, it has led me to believe that the role of many high executives is overrated. Executives tend to get credit for anything that happens on their watch. It often means they get credit they do not deserve, and the hierarchical organizational system seems more effective than it really is. I remember the résumé of a Design Division director who left for a more exalted administrative position at another university. The section listing his administrative achievements showed that, during his directorship, the Design Division budget had tripled. He neglected to mention that the entire increase was due to research grants the faculty had obtained, and that he had had absolutely no part in either raising or spending the money. I don't fault him; I would have done the same thing.

I also notice how having one person at the head of a group causes bottlenecks. If it is a hierarchical system, leaders need to be available, or things have to wait for them. If the leader is wrong, then the entire enterprise can be brought to ruin. There is a long-standing argument for the idea that one person needs to be in charge. It goes way back to Adam Smith's writings in *The Wealth of Nations*. Even Friedrich Engels agreed with Smith that "a ship needs one captain."

I certainly am not an expert on ships, and I hate to disagree with the luminaries of both capitalism and communism, however, this is at variance with my experience. The flat, participatory model we developed worked very well and completely suited my personality. I feel blessed to have worked under it for the main part of my career at Stanford.

I can assure you that the model we developed worked better than the conventional alternatives that abound at Stanford. I strongly encourage readers in academia, industry, and other fields to experiment and find an appropriate model for your own situations. If you can break the thrall of the conventional wisdom, you might find a management structure that strongly supports what you want to accomplish.

MINIMIZING COMPETITION

You may not have a choice in how a group is led. Whenever there is a hierarchy of positions and pay scales, it's likely that you'll also encounter some people who will step on each other as they attempt to climb the ladder.

You'll know them as the office gossips, the backstabbers, the users, the phonies. I encourage you to steer clear of this entire culture. I can't tell you that people like that don't wind up in high positions; they do, and too often. It is important to ask yourself what kind of satisfaction you'll derive from being that kind of person, even if it does mean you get the title you want. Don't lose sight of your humanity in the pursuit of a fancier car.

Many businesses and academic organizations use competition as a means of encouraging people to do their best—they literally have contests (sales contests, design contests, etc.) pitting people against each other. Although our culture is habituated to winner-take-all athletics and other zero-sum games, I'm not a fan of this. While it can have a strong upside for the winner, it has a strong downside for everyone else. It can lower morale, foster jealousy, and hurt relationships.

It's important to learn to be motivated to do your personal best, regardless of what happens around you. I have found that contests bring out the worst in students, whereas learning to cooperate and share brings out the best.

If students are exposed to a learning environment where there is a strong mutually supportive teaching team as role models, and if they are given enough autonomy, they generate their own sense of excitement and commitment without the defeat and discouragement that is an inherent part of the contest mode. It is generally believed that contests are good motivators. I agree that they are, however, they are not the only motivators. We regularly get extremely high student motivation for—and draw large crowds of spectators to—project presentations that are the result of cooperation rather than competition.[4] The positive motivational effects are just as good, without the destructive downside of contests.

Look for ways to be inclusive rather than competitive—for ways to help the whole team win rather than just one individual. As much as possible, it behooves you to erase the idea of competition in the workplace from your mind. Competition leads to backstabbing, gossip, and generally negative feelings, even if you succeed at what you set out to accomplish. Maybe you'll get the raise, however, you'll also lose friendships, and may ever after feel that you have to watch your back.

Power dynamics often lead to this competition. When there are multiple levels or layers in an organization, you may have a boss, and a boss's boss, and so on. Maybe a coworker has more clout than you do, or is making more money.

This is all meaningless. In life—*real* life—none of that matters. You have to be satisfied only with yourself—not worried about what the Joneses are up to.

One great way that we get rid of power struggles is by going for walks together. See, if I have a meeting with a colleague in my office, then I'm the one with power, and vice versa if the meeting is in her office. Instead we walk. The hierarchy is gone.

Whenever you can, eliminate situations in which one person is sitting behind a desk. The desk creates distance and a power imbalance that can make the other person feel self-conscious and "less than." Meet on neutral ground as equals.

RETHINKING A PRIVATE OFFICE

In the Engineering School at Stanford every professor has a closed-off room known as his private office. I had the standard relationship with my private office for forty-three years, and I was happy with the situation.

My office housed my vast collection of books, theses, and offprints of technical papers. It also housed all my paper files and was decorated with framed pictures of a long-ago trip to Chiapas, Mexico. In addition there was a collection of mechanical models that I used in my lectures, to amuse visitors and to remind me of some past experience. Then I got involved in the d.school, and my relationship to my office changed.

There are no private offices at the d.school, just open bull-pen arrangements. It was like the space I shared with other lecturers at the City College of New York when I had my first teaching job, and the space I shared with other PhD students at Columbia University. It is hardly the prestigious office that a chaired senior full professor expects. Yet I found that I spent more and more time in the d.school staff space and less and less in my private office.

This arrangement went on for over four years. Then two major events occurred in my life. After four moves, the d.school finally landed in its permanent home, and the building that held my private Mechanical Engineering Design Group office was condemned. A new, smaller private office was assigned to me in a separate wing of the same building that now houses the d.school.

I donated my collection of books and research documents to a special library at the University of California–Davis and moved the rest of my possessions into my new private office. I hardly ever go there. Instead I lend it to individuals with critical space needs. I spend all my time at the d.school.

At the d.school there are now not even partitions between people's spaces; a staff of more than twenty shares one common, unobstructed space outfitted with a few desks, many shelflike desktops, portable files, and desktop computers. There is no hierarchy that determines who sits where, and there is periodic spontaneous shifting of home bases.

When we first moved into the permanent d.school space, we had just hired a woman named Kim to be our chief financial person. Previously, she had worked for many years in the dean's office, and she was very familiar with the Stanford finance system. After two weeks she told me that she was finding it difficult to do her work in the open d.school space. I immediately responded that I could solve her problem. We purchased a new desktop computer for her and set her up in my private office. I gave her my office key and assured her she would be the only person using that office.

After about ten days I noticed Kim was back at her original computer station in the open-space community office; she never went back to the private office. Once she had experienced the feelings of camaraderie, she could not go back to the old seclusion of the private office; it was too isolating for her. I knew just how she felt. We eventually moved the computer out of the private office and into our common space. (I wonder if the computer also felt a sense of relief.)

Before we moved to the open floor plan, I had been in private offices my entire professional life. I now realize how much better equipped the d.school is for individual and group relations. It also does wonders for information flow and communications. When I come in to work, it feels very much like coming home to my family.

We do, of course, all have times when we need to think or work without interruptions. When that happens, there's a simple signal: we put on headphones, and then everyone knows not to bother us. We can also remove ourselves from that space and go into one of the private rooms if we need quiet.

If you have any input into your work space, try opening it up to a more nonhierarchical setup. Give yourself some time to get used to it, and then see if you work better in a collaborative environment.

SPACE AND BODY LANGUAGE

Physical position is very important. Unless I am giving a theater-style lecture, my favorite teaching arrangement is to have everyone sit in a circle. Moreover, I insist on the circle being as small and as perfectly round as possible. The closer the people are to each other physically, the better the group functions. I have conducted many experiments with all sorts of groups, and the results are overwhelmingly in favor of very tight circles. This falls in line with the design thinking concept of radical collaboration—a circle means there's no hierarchy of who sits where. There are no "good seats," "bad seats," or preconceived notions about the types of people who sit in front (brown-nosers) or back (class clowns and slackers). It means that we're all looking at each other, encouraging eye contact and connections among people.

Changing the circle's diameter changes the feeling in the group in a very palpable way. If we want everyone to participate, then no one can be left out physically; everyone needs to be on the same level. If someone sits back a little from the circumference, she is left out emotionally as well as physically. And those too far inside exclude others by blocking their view of fellow participants.

If you find yourself on the periphery of a group and notice that you feel left out, try moving to a more central location; chances are you will feel more involved in what is going on. Change your location, and you will change how you feel about the event you're attending. When you have trouble really engaging or working on a goal, see if your location is supporting or hindering your efforts. It's hard to get noticed at work if you're always sitting closest to the exit, and it's more likely you'll put in more effort in your workout class if you're in the instructor's sight line.

I am often in a situation in which students working on the same project sit in a group of four or more around a small table. If one of the students does not seem to be participating much, and her chair is farther away from the table than the other students, I gently push that student's chair inward so that she is physically an integral part of the group. That change usually results in much greater participation from the former outlier. Be aware of your body and what it is telling you. If you like what it is saying, keep doing what you are doing. If you do not like what it is saying, move it to the position where it says what you like.

Large meetings provide classic examples of the importance of physical position. They often take place in conference rooms where there is one big rectangular table that everyone sits around. If the table is long, it is difficult to see most of the people on your side of the table. If people do not see each other, the effectiveness of their communication is diminished. If one person is running the meeting, or perceived as more important than the others, there is an implicit authority associated with how close you sit to that person.

If you want to strengthen your voice in the meeting, sit as close to the authority figure(s) as possible and opposite the people you want to influence. If you want to hide, sit on the same side of the table and as far as possible from the people you want to hide from. It is even easier to disappear if the room is so crowded that you can take a back-row seat and not sit at the table at all. If you have no one to hide from and you want to have a fully participatory meeting, it is much better to abandon the rectangular conference table in favor of a circular arrangement where everyone can see and be seen by all of the other participants. Your physical position at a meeting influences both your effectiveness and your state of mind.

Working in a supportive physical environment is a huge plus, as students in the Stanford d.school know well. A book about the school, *Make Space* (Doorley and Witthoft, 2012), refers to some of the key factors in providing a space to promote creative learning in learning-by-doing situations.

It is interesting to look at attitudes about the d.school type of space. People seeing it for the first time immediately think of it as being a "creative space." So do the students. It is as if the space is talking to them, saying, "Hey, the expectations here are different from those in the rest of the university."

When we were designing the space, there were often arguments between the d.school team and the people who manage space renovations for the university. I recall being told several times, "It may be good for you guys, but who will want to use it if you leave the building?" It turns out almost everyone wants it.

TAKE CONTROL OF YOUR ENVIRONMENT

The question of spatial position and body language is widely neglected in education. Most of university education is set up to be teacher- and mind-centered. The major concern seems to be whether the students can see and hear the lecturer. There is little regard for student-to-student communication; the idea that a student's spatial position might influence the quality of her education gets little recognition.

A simple experiment brings home the importance of body position. In any group setting, take a moment of silence and become mindful of your emotional state. Then change your position within the group, take a moment of silence again, and notice your new emotional state.

This experiment can be done with any size group participating simultaneously. It is amazing what a difference even small changes of position can make.

YOUR TURN

The next time you are in a meeting that is not working, get your group to rearrange their chairs in a circle and see what happens. Asking each person in turn to say something (anything he wants to say, as long as it is only a few words or a short sentence) is an excellent way to start each meeting. It is also a great way to end each meeting. This works especially well if people are seated in a close circle.

One of my profound learning experiences about body positions occurred when I was teaching my "Introduction to Robotics" course in a large auditorium. There were about ninety students in a space that could seat four hundred. The students sat all over the auditorium, and most of them chose to sit toward the back. I repeatedly requested, during the first few weeks, that they sit toward the front when they came for the next class—they never did.

The class met three times a week for fifty-minute sessions, and I noticed that I was exhausted after each lecture. Even though I used a microphone, it felt like I was being drained by trying to reach this widely distributed mass of students. So I got a roll of yellow barricade tape, the type with large black letters reading CAUTION. I went into the auditorium a half hour before class and taped off the entire back half of the room. When the students arrived they naturally migrated to the front, and were even further biased toward the first few rows. Who would want to sit close to the taped-off section, with its unknown dangers?

I ended that lecture with more energy than when I started. Instead of the students draining me, I was being energized by this captive mass of people who I could now easily interact with. They were there with me, and I could give to them and get from them. I repeated the taping for two weeks. After that the students were habituated to their new seats, and I did not need to close off the back.

That was a long time ago, and I will always remember that class and those students with a special fondness. I am still very pleased with myself that I took control of the physical situation and didn't just tough it out and suffer through ten weeks of a debilitating experience.

The meta-lesson here is, take control of your environment. If you are leading a meeting, or if your goal is to learn to give a successful presentation, give some thought to everybody's position. If you are in a meeting or listening to a lecture and you feel bored or left out, move to the front. If you feel intimidated, go hide at the back. If you are distracted by the person next to you, or cannot hear or see, move. Be mindful of how you feel, and experiment by moving to different locations. Our body's location matters. It colors our experience more than most of us think.

THE MIND-BODY CONNECTION

My wife, Ruth, two close friends, and I were in a small single-engine plane on a long, slow flight over California's Imperial Valley. We were playing cards to entertain ourselves. The pilot had turned on the autopilot and rotated his seat so he could play with us. The game went on for about forty minutes, and suddenly there was a click, followed by a frightening silence. The engine had stopped firing. In a flash the pilot spun his seat around, cards flying in the air. He flipped the switch to the other gas tank, and the engine started up again immediately. He reacted reflexively without any analysis. He had been trained so that his body reacted; he did not need to pause and think. It was incredibly impressive, and we were glad we had him as our pilot. Still, we did not resume our card game for the rest of the trip.

There are movement activities that directly use the mind-body connection to stimulate learning and creativity. In the Design Division, we have been teaching these activities for a long time. Originally, these were considered somewhat New

Agey. I recall an unlucky lecturer getting into a lot of trouble when he broke an ankle doing a warm-up exercise. The president's office could not see any justification for an engineering design class being in the women's gym for warm-up exercises. Fortunately, those days are long past.

Dance and all forms of body movement are also valuable for working and learning in groups. You have probably been at events where a speaker has asked the audience to stand up for a minute and stretch. Just a simple interlude of stretching can make a huge difference in your ability to properly participate and to think creatively.

The human body needs to move. It likes to move, and it loves to move to music. When we introduce movement into our classes and workshops, the response is overwhelmingly positive, even from participants with special physical limitations.

In the intensive weeklong "Introduction to Design Thinking" workshop we did at the d.school each summer, we programmed two half-hour movement sessions each day, led by a professional dance teacher: one in the morning and one in the afternoon. The sessions did not require any special training, just the ability to go with the flow and join the pandemonium of forty bodies moving to loud music. The energy level rose after each such session, and everyone was ready to conquer whatever came next. The effect of the movement sessions on the workshop atmosphere was palpable through the entire day. It was in sharp contrast to workshops where people just sit and talk.

In my experience, most people take readily to such physical activities as part of their learning and work process. Even people who are at first reluctant to participate quickly overcome their hesitation and join the fun. The big secret, though, is that this stuff is more than fun. It is actually a great way to give your mind what it needs: the mind-body connection. Whenever possible, include extra movement activities in your schedule.

SEEING WITH YOUR BODY

My wife, Ruth, uses all her senses to learn about her environment. She is always touching, feeling, smelling, looking, and listening to things. Like a child, she often gets into trouble touching stuff she shouldn't. I will never forget when eight guards came running at us from all directions at the Rijksmuseum in Amsterdam. Ruth had set off the alarm by using her hand to "see" the canvas on a Rembrandt painting.

My mode of learning, by contrast, is primarily cerebral. It is enough for me to deal with the concept; I do not need to touch something to know what it is. I can imagine objects in my head. Ruth cannot visualize in her head; she has to touch and see the real thing. When we discuss rearranging the furniture, I can visualize the change. She cannot. We need to move the furniture so that she can see the concept, then after experiencing all possible configurations, she is much better than I am at seeing what works best.

When we did a house remodel, we put just enough detail in the plans to get the building permits. The plans were a placeholder. The real design took place during construction, when Ruth had the workers physically lay out various different ideas. The builder's accountant loved it!

Ruth is an artist and a born craftsperson and tinkerer. She has fantastic talent for making and fixing things, and she is continually using her physical senses to learn. She truly learns by doing. We have some students at Stanford with similar dispositions, who unfortunately are the exceptions; the admission system creates a bias toward other types of learning. Happily, a maker culture has been growing in popularity, and every year hundreds more students get exposed to a balanced approach in which they learn with their entire bodies, not only with their heads. This fits well with the design thinking method of ideating; it's a way of opening yourself up to new possibilities by allowing your brain to experience problem solving in ways you normally wouldn't.

BLIND WALKS

A good way to become aware of your body's ability to see and learn is to disrupt the usual use of your senses. A blind walk is an easy exercise that is both enjoyable and informative.

The blind walk can have various forms. The form I use most often is to have two people work as partners. The main rule is that they cannot talk to each other during the exercise. One partner stays "blind"—closing his eyes or using a blindfold—for a period of thirty minutes or more. After that time, the partners switch roles without talking, and the other person stays "blind" for an equal amount of time. Then they both open their eyes and can talk. Because this is a group activity, they also debrief with the entire group.

The idea is that the "sighted" person acts as a guide for the blind person. Usually the sighted person's job is to facilitate an exploration that will stimulate the blind person's other senses. This helps the person explore the environment in new ways, using the senses of touch, hearing, taste, and smell. Once in an interesting spot, it is important that the guide gives the blind person a lot of freedom and yet maintains responsibility for his safety, staying aware of his desires and sensibilities. Does he prefer to play it safe and move cautiously, for example, or would he like to run and climb trees while blind?

Most of the time the guide should not lead the blind person by the hand. Most leading can easily be done hands-off, using mainly the sense of sound. It is very easy for the blind person to follow the sound of the leader's steps, snapping fingers, or tapping on objects.

This exercise promotes sensory awareness and opens up new ways of "seeing" the world. I once spent a weekend with my eyes closed. My guide and I went to restaurants and supermarkets, played catch, rode in cars and in an airplane, and even bicycled. My insights were much deeper and different from those I had gotten from short blind-walk exercises.

The next time you're feeling stuck, take a blind walk or change your sensory inputs in another way. Chances are, this will help you to achieve what you are after. Even if it doesn't, you will learn to "see" the world differently by using your body in new ways, and you will have new sensibilities and richer perceptual experiences.

IMPROVISATION

Improvisation, or improv, is an art form originally associated with the theater. In recent years at Stanford it has spread from its home in the drama department into many parts of the university. Improv directly involves the body and enhances spontaneity, observation, communication, and other vital skills. In addition, many of the common improv warm-up exercises are excellent analogues for problem-solving skills, and as such make excellent teaching tools. One of my favorites is called Word-Ball.

Before doing Word-Ball for the first time, it is good to introduce it to a group without its members using words. First, just have them practice tossing an imaginary ball. A group of six to twelve people form a circle, and one player starts by tossing an imaginary ball to another player. The receiving player catches the imaginary ball and immediately tosses it to another player.

The objective is to have the imaginary ball moving all the time. The learning starts at this point. Some people do not pay attention, so they either never get the ball thrown to them, or they miss it if it is. Other people clown it up. This may be funny, but mainly it just stops the action and slows down the ball. This warm-up is a great analogue to many forms of group activities, such as brainstorming, meetings, and conversations.

Once the group gets the hang of throwing the ball, it is time to introduce a word. Now, in addition to throwing the imaginary ball, the player throws a word out as he throws the ball to another player. The catching player repeats the word she has caught and then immediately, without forethought, throws a different word. The objective of the game is to keep words (and the ball) moving among players as quickly as possible.

Players have to learn to trust in their spontaneity and stay focused on the game, which tests how well they maintain their attention on their intention to catch and throw words. Now, in addition to the pitfalls mentioned for the practice without words, we add the difficulty of people's inability to be spontaneous in generating a word; many people do not trust their own abilities to respond in real time.

If you stay in your head instead of the game, you will not really be participating in group activities—not just in Word-Ball but also in brainstorming, meetings, and conversations.

There are many variations of Word-Ball. You can have Sound-Ball, where you throw and receive sounds. You can have Theme-Ball, where you throw and receive words related to a certain theme (for example, water). You can have Concept-Ball, where you throw and receive short concepts related to a certain theme (for example, if the theme is water, someone can say "conservation"). The variations are endless. I find that, in all cases, the best learning comes from using the same basic ground rules: keep the ball moving, stay in the game, be spontaneous (don't stockpile), and be a team player.

It is also common, once the group gets warmed up and performing well, to introduce a second and even a third ball, so there are multiple ball throwers and catchers at the same time. Although I find it less appealing, it is also possible to use a real softball or other physical object such as a knotted towel instead of the imaginary ball.

The practice of improv has a set of commandments, the two most relevant of which for our purposes are "Yes, and" and "No blocking." Let's give them a try!

YOUR TURN

Two people partner, and one leads off with a suggested action. The other then must reply: "Yes, and . . . ," accepting the original suggestion and building upon it to keep the story going. The first person then makes another suggestion, and they keep building. The net result is forward movement of ideas and a fun feeling of collaboration.

For example:

First person: Let's have a party tomorrow.

Second person: Yes, and let's invite a lot of people.

First person: Let's have music.

Second person: Yes, and dancing too.

Blocking is another term used in improv. When you are blocking, you stop the flow of action and creative movement. The partner says no to every suggestion, or gives a reason why it will not be a good idea, or brings up something entirely at odds with the original suggestion. The net result is the generation of a blockage with no way of moving ahead. This is a downer; it generates feelings of opposition rather than collaboration.

> For example:
>
> First person: Let's have a party tomorrow.
>
> Second person: No, I hate parties.
>
> First person: Let's have music.
>
> Second person: No, I don't like music either.

The applicability of these rules to all sorts of problem solving and human interaction is obvious. The recognition of the broad utility of improv concepts has taken the art form into many areas beyond its origins in theater and storytelling. It is worthwhile incorporating improv ideas into your professional and personal lives.

STREAKING

You know what streaking is, don't you? It's when someone runs naked in public, intending to be noticed. What does that have to do with the topic of this chapter? Well, it has everything to do with it for me. Why else would I have put it in? I use the word *streaking* not in the naked sense but instead as a method of unusual disruption that charges the energy level where a group is working.

In the 1970s I was about thirty minutes into a tedious lecture on mechanical vibrations to a very bored class of seniors. Suddenly the door opened and a naked man entered, ran one lap around the classroom, and left without a word.

The energy level in the room went from -10 to +80. (Don't ask me what the units on these numbers are, or how I measured them; we'll just call it the Bernie Scale.) I was amazed that when we all recovered and I resumed the lecture, it seemed like a different class. My speaking became energized, and the students' attention improved significantly. And even better, that change lasted. Four weeks were left in the term, and they went much better than the first six weeks. The streaker had changed my course for the better.

After this experience I understood the beneficial effects of random interruptions to classes. The more bizarre the event, the better it is. I call them *streaks* in honor of the first time it happened to me with the actual streaker. Most people do not like interruptions to their lectures or workshops. I have learned to welcome and cherish them as random gifts.

If I notice the energy level in a group or class is low, I can declare a break at any time. In fact, it is not uncommon for me to ask a group to stand up and take a stretch or go on a short break. As useful as these activities are, though, they do not hold the same energy charge as when an outside interruption blesses you with a streak.

Unfortunately, streaks are rather rare, unless you are devious and arrange for them yourself. So the best I have been willing to do is use the *concept* of streaking to give myself permission to be honest about what is going on in the room.

I no longer ignore it or try to hide the truth from myself or my classes: if I feel I am being boring, I stop talking. If I feel the energy level in the room is low, I point it out to the group and do something about it. For me the gift of the streaks has brought a greater willingness to be responsible for the energy and attention level whenever I am with people, regardless of whether it is a class, a meeting, or simply people working together in a group.

Working well in a team requires you to be flexible and tolerant. Changing the physical surroundings and doing group exercises can help the team be more cohesive and effective at problem solving. Even when your group is all about "business," leaving room for play can only improve the working environment and boost productivity.

SELF-
IMAGE
BY DESIGN

CHAPTER 8

Always certain; often wrong.

—Anonymous

Stanford's d.school has become famous for methodologies centered on using collaborative approaches to inspire human-centered innovations. We always ask: Who are the people we are solving the problem for, and what do they want and need? Human-centered interactions (which mean that people come first) are at the heart of our work because we have found that the achievement of almost any dream relies on our ability to infuse empathy into the project. Usually we think about empathy in terms of getting to know strangers or outside groups so we can understand them better, and thus assist them with some of their needs. We can also turn the idea of empathy inward, using it to better understand ourselves, our friends, our families, and the people we work with.

What you can achieve in life has a lot to do with your self-image. If you see yourself as a risk taker and a doer, you're more likely to take risks and do! If you see yourself as cautious and scared, it may make the road to achieving your goals a lot more protracted and difficult. You may not even know for sure how you define yourself, so let's figure out where your self-image comes from and if it suits where you want to be.

EXAMINE YOUR ROLE MODELS

When we are young, we learn from those around us. Naturally, our parents and siblings have a strong influence on who we become as we start to mature. We may be very fortunate and start life in a warm, supporting environment. We may be less fortunate, and start in a harsh threatening environment. Whether we grow up feeling accepted and loved by our family or harshly judged and rejected, it is almost impossible to escape those imprints. We may turn out to be very similar to our family members, or very different; either way, they have influenced us in many subtle ways. They are normally the first people who teach us what and how we are supposed to achieve in life.

When my younger son was five years old, a doctor asked him if he preferred to take an antibiotic in the form of pills or an injection. His reply was, "Whichever is cheaper." Clearly, he already had picked up an attitude toward money from his parents. Now, at age fifty-five, he still has the same attitude toward spending money.

I believe I am very different from my father, and my wife believes she is very different from her mother. Still, the most hurtful thing my wife can say to me is, "You are just like your father"; and I can deliver an equally upsetting blow by telling her she is just like her mother.

In truth, we both carry some of our parents with us, in spite of our desire not to. We deny having the traits that we did not like in our parents, even if it is obvious we do share some of those traits. On the other hand, the things we liked about our parents we more willingly accept as part of our inheritance, even when there is little evidence that we actually share them.

YOUR TURN

Examine your family's viewpoints and how they have affected your adult life.

- What do they think about money?
- What do they think is a suitable life path for you?
- What are their views on authority?
- What are their views on hard work? Grades? Blue-collar versus white-collar work? Getting ahead in life? Work versus play? Hobbies? Taking risks professionally and personally? Personal fulfillment?
- Which of their views do you agree with, and which don't you? Have you tailored your life in response to their views? Is it helpful to you, harmful, or neutral? Which influences of theirs are better off discarded? Which can you learn from?

On the way to maturity, we go through several stages. The first big break from the nuclear family typically occurs when we enter school and must learn to deal with strangers without the protection of parents or their surrogates. We need to learn to face challenges, competition, frustrations, and the judgment of peers. Schoolmates can be unkind, and we may face physical violence or ridicule.

It is in this environment that we first get to look at ourselves and start to form a self-image that reflects who we are rather than who our parents think we are. If we are lucky, we find a kindred spirit who is usually much like us and becomes our closest friend. This friend becomes a way to know ourselves better because we are free to share things that we withhold from our parents. With the right friend we are free to explore new aspects of ourselves in a supportive situation as we test and expand the world around us.

In the teenage years this need for intimacy in friendship becomes more diffuse, and more friends enter the circle. This further removes us from our parents, and provides an opportunity for developing and testing our self-image in a new and uncertain environment. It may involve exploration and experimentation into new realms such as sex and drugs. It certainly involves a strong redefinition of self and very strong peer pressure to take on group characteristics. If as adolescents we find a kindred group, our sense of belonging to this world is solidified. If not, it is possible that we might suffer a life of alienation and isolation. Fortunately, most people survive their adolescent traumas, and some are strengthened and made highly self-reliant and resourceful by the experience.

My mother died when I was twelve years old, and my father suffered from a severe manic-depressive disorder. Basically, I was on my own during my teenage years. I held a lot of different after-school and summer jobs, roamed New York City widely, owned cars and motorcycles before I was old enough for a driver's license, and got into trouble in and out of school. I believe these experiences made me more autonomous and capable than I would have been if I had received the same degree of parental guidance as most of my peers.

In addition to the personal, lifelong sense of loss associated with not having my mother, the downside of being on my own was that I received my guidance from the people on the street.

Not everything they advised was wise or legal. My high school choice was basically made by Charlie, a senior playing football for Stuyvesant High School. I still recall his words of wisdom, "Go to Stuyvesant; you're not smart enough to get into Bronx Science."

I allowed guys like Charlie to define the limits of what I could achieve. I could beat myself up for that. I am wiser now, and can look back on my earlier years with empathy for my former self and realize that I had a lot going on in my life emotionally, and that I had not yet figured out who I was or what I wanted.

I prefer not to think of the past with regret. We all have things we're not particularly proud of, yet we can't let that fact hover over what we are capable of achieving now. It takes time to gain perspective, particularly during those formative years when we're testing our self-image against how we see other people. We must be kind to ourselves.

As we leave our teenage years, the next big event in forming self-image occurs when we make a special bond with a love interest. The end result of this pairing is often marriage or some equivalent cohabitation with a partner, and a de facto moving away from the larger group of friends.[1] In addition, this is usually a period of personal growth, in which we learn and enhance our marketable skills. We now develop a newer version of our self-image, integrating the influences from our intimate pairing and our skills training into our pictures of ourselves as autonomous adults.

In my case this manifested itself when I got married at the end of my junior year in college. I started to teach as a lecturer after I graduated the following year, and I did graduate work in the afternoons and evenings. Eventually I earned a PhD and obtained an assistant professorship at Stanford University.

BECOMING AUTONOMOUS

College and university professors are not usually trained how to teach; they're trained to be researchers and to mimic what their teachers have done. It can take many years before they find their own voice as teachers. To some extent they never shake the influence of their professors entirely, just as one is never entirely free of parental (or parental surrogates') influences.

I had just led a full-day workshop in Taiwan titled "Creative Teaching," and a young assistant professor was driving me back to my hotel. In the privacy of the car he told me, "That was very interesting. I never thought that I could modify how I teach. I did not realize I could consider redesigning the structure of my job and actually approach the issue of how to teach as a problem-solving activity." He was visibly shaken: he had seen a yellow-eyed cat. He now understood that teaching needs to be approached from an individual perspective that is broader than simply covering specific material; teachers need to be clear what their intention is for each class session, and develop a style suited to who they are.

Unfortunately, many people are in the same trap—and not only in academia. We are influenced by our teachers and parents to the extent that we spend our lives trying, as best we can, to mimic them, and all too often we end up being second-rate replicas.

One of the social functions of families and the other communities to which we belong is to constrain our behavior. Normally these social constraints serve a valid societal function. Yet they can also have a big downside unless we are willing to confront and—if appropriate—discard them in a productive manner. If we realize we have a unique persona and a history different from that of our teachers and parents, we can end up being creators of a new synthesis that honors our influences yet is also a true expression of our very being. It is important that we look at our life and work not only from the point of view of its content but also from the question of what our actual intentions are.

YOUR TURN

Create a list of all the things you intend to accomplish with your work. You can get there by asking yourself a series of questions:

What is my intention?

Is it simply to get through the day?

Is it to get a specific task done?

Is it to have a good time?

Is it to bolster my ego?

Is it to delight?

Is it to inspire?

Is it to motivate?

Is it to escape?

Then, once it is clear what your basic intentions are, the next issue is how to accomplish them. Before you get to that, it is important to be sure your intentions are real and not simply a series of clichés that you have been programmed to recite or have created to appease your self-image. Once you have your basic intentions clear, you can view the method of implementing them as a creative problem-solving activity that will get you unshackled from past practices and mimicked constraints.

If we are with someone we admire, we often start to take on some of her traits. In this way we learn how to act from our parents, romantic partners, friends, teachers, and colleagues. Generally this happens subconsciously. Interestingly, it is also possible to learn from them how *not* to be; this generally requires some conscious effort. For example, if I grow up in a house where my parents are continually fighting or mad at each other, I can note that it is something I do not want to replicate in my own family. However, unless I specifically guard against it, my parents' behavior will likely surface in me when the going gets tough with my spouse.

HOW YOU SEE YOURSELF

In our minds we all have pictures of what and who we are; these are collectively known as our self-image. Our interpretations of our self-image—that of our bodies, emotions, actions, and thoughts—ultimately define for us who we are. We may have an accurate self-image, or it may be way off the mark.

YOUR TURN

List five short (one- or two-word) descriptors of the type of person you think you are. Ask five friends or family members to each also list five things that describe who they think you are. Then compare their twenty-five items with your five items. The amount of agreement and disagreement can give you valuable insights regarding the accuracy of your self-image.

Whether or not we have an accurate self-image, it can strongly color who we are, what we do, and how we respond to the world around us. Others can use it to manipulate us, and we can use it to manipulate others. It can be largely positive or largely negative, though for most people it is both.

Often our self-image constrains what we will and will not do, or at least colors our feelings about what we have and have not done. In an ideal world, self-image would form the basis for much of what we did and didn't do; in the real world, things are a bit more complicated. Using rationalization, people can justify any action or inaction in an attempt to bring it into accord with their self-image.

Most of us do not have a completely realistic self-image. Harvard business psychologist Chris Argyris concluded, after forty years of studying people, that they "consistently act inconsistently, unaware of the contradiction . . . between the way they think they are acting and the way they really act."[2] Causing our behavior to fall in line with our self-image requires telling ourselves the truth, not lying to ourselves or rationalizing our behavior. Our self-image evolves and changes as we go through life. We may have certain inborn tendencies that get reinforced by our environment, while entirely new aspects come as the result of our experiences as we accumulate successes and failures. Thus one of the ways we can change our behavior is to proactively change our self-image while at the same time bringing our behavior in line with our self-image. In fully integrated people, behavior changes self-image and self-image changes behavior throughout their lives.

In the Stanford d.school we attempt to bring students through a series of experiences that change their self-image so that they think of themselves as being more creative. We call this boosting their *creative confidence.*[3] Michael Jensen, Werner Erhard, and their associates use a similar concept in leadership training; they call it "changing the context." Others call these types of changes "reframing" or "changing frameworks." Whatever it is called, the psychological milieu in which we operate is important because it acts as a hidden arbitrator in how we approach many aspects of our lives. The Your Turn exercises in this chapter are designed to assist in exploring and expanding the bounds of your self-image.

YOUR TURN

One way to look at your self-image is to make a list of your attributes. This can be done by again answering the question "Who am I?" In order to gain deeper insight, however, this time you will look at who you are in a way that contrasts the "being" part of your self-image to the parts involving your possessions and your activities. As suggested in the "Use Your Brain" section at the end of chapter 1, each question should be repeated for at least five or ten minutes. If you have someone available to work with, you can take turns where one person repeatedly asks the same question and the other person answers. Of course, if there are two people, the questions need to be rephrased: "Who are you?"

- Who am I in terms of what I have?
- Who am I in terms of what I do?
- Who am I in terms of my being?

This exercise gives you a chance to stop the daily chatter in your head and to look separately at what you have, what you do, and who you are. It gives you an opportunity to dig deep and see how your life is stacking up compared to your self-image. It can give you a midcourse correction or reaffirm that you are sailing in the desired direction.

People often confuse who they are with their possessions, their achievements, or their jobs. The parsing of the question into three parts thus helps them to gain clarity. Every time I do this exercise, I am reminded it is more subtle than it first appears. For example, in terms of what I have, I could say a wife, two sons, a professorship, a house, friends, students and former students, several bicycles, a newly completed book manuscript, and hundreds of research papers. In terms of what I do I might come up with husbanding, parenting, teaching and research, household tasks, socializing, mentoring and relating, cycling, driving, writing, and publishing. The two lists are more or less identical.

None of this informs who I am in terms of my being. Or does it?

Much depends on how I relate to these things. Teaching, for example, is for some people a thing they *have*; the teaching job is their proudest possession. I remember how astounded I was when I accompanied one of my professors to pick up his dry cleaning and the clerk addressed him as "doctor" and later also as "professor." This was at some mom-and-pop establishment in Flushing, New York, ten miles—and light-years—away from Columbia University. This is common in Europe, yet it seemed comically out of place in the context of a working-class neighborhood in New York City. It actually reinforced my sense that the poor fellow was using his job to hide who he really was.

To some people, teaching is something they *do*. It is a job, pure and simple. That job is like any other job to them: they go to work, put in their time, and get paid; the job is purely instrumental. They work to have money to pay rent, feed their family, and subscribe to cable television.

Other people are born to teach. If they did not have teaching jobs they would still be teachers. It is their calling, an intimate part of their being. I remember reading in one of Henry Miller's early books that he and all of his friends knew he was a writer even though, at the time, he was working as a messenger and had not yet published anything.

So, depending on how I hold it, teaching could be something I have, or something I do, or part of my very being. The same is true for many things in people's lives. There is no right answer as to what category something belongs in. It all depends on you. It is important, however, to know the difference, and not to confuse what you have or what you do with who you are. Knowing this increases your chances of forming a valid self-image.

Some people's self-image totally identifies them with their origins. One such person is my good friend Bruno. More than most people's, Bruno's life is punctuated by adventures, which in turn are fueled by his rock-solid self-image of being a Neapolitan alpha male. This became clear to me many years ago during a conference in Linz, Austria. Several of us had gone to a disco after dinner. There were some local women sitting next to us, and Bruno asked one of them to dance. She declined, and Bruno could not believe it. He exclaimed loudly, "But I am Italian. I am from Naples!"

He did not give up but kept asking her to dance, and she steadfastly refused in spite of what he thought to be his impeccable credentials. Soon he switched tactics and started engaging her in conversation. I lost interest and did not follow along. When we left the disco, Bruno triumphantly showed me a piece of paper, saying, "She gave me her phone number." Alas, the next day when he dialed the number, he was amazed to find it was not valid. He was sure there had been an error in transcription. He could not imagine what seemed obvious to the rest of us: that she had given him a made-up number to get rid of him. I am certain she made an error, though not the one Bruno thinks she made. Her error was in not writing down her actual number. Bruno is right—he's a lot of fun!

A good tool to assist in looking at who we really are is called *guided fantasy*. We do this by closing our eyes and creating a fantasy experience in which we examine some surrogate entity such as a tree or a house. Then we give a detailed description of what we have seen in our fantasy. Finally we repeat the description, this time in the voice of the surrogate object. In this way we gain access to images of ourselves that we generally hide or are not consciously aware of.

YOUR TURN

Guided fantasy is a good tool to assist you in examining who you really are. The script I use follows. You can record yourself reading it and then lie down on the floor or any flat surface and follow its instructions as you listen to the recording.

Please close your eyes. Become aware of your breath going in and out. Notice the air temperature. Notice your chest expanding and contracting.

Take your awareness from your chest to the right side of your body. Put your awareness on your right hip. Now move it down along the front of your leg to the front of your right knee. Now take your awareness down along your shin to your right ankle. Go across the top of your right foot to your smallest toe. Take your awareness across the toes on your right foot to the big toe, then up the inside of your right leg to your crotch and then to your belly. Take your awareness to your left hip. Now move it down along the front of your left leg to the front of your left knee. Now take your awareness down along your shin to your left ankle. Go across the top of your left foot to your smallest toe. Take your awareness across the toes on your left foot to the big toe, then up the inside of your left leg to your crotch and then to your belly.

Now take your awareness up your chest to your chin. Be aware of your breath going in and out. Notice the air temperature. Notice your chest expanding and contracting.

Now imagine you are going to take a journey. Imagine standing up and going to the airport. Imagine boarding a plane for a short flight. Imagine getting off the plane and making your way to a bus. Take a short bus ride, and then imagine getting off the bus. Now, imagine a house in the distance, and walk toward that house. When you get to the house, explore the outside and then the inside, examining the details carefully.

(Ten-minute pause here.)

Get ready to leave the house and make your return trip.

First walk back to where you got off the bus. Imagine the bus returning, and take it back to the airport. Board a plane and fly back to your original airport. Then make your way back to this room.

Imagine that you lie down again. Become aware of your breathing, aware of your breath going in and out. Notice the air temperature. Notice your chest expanding and contracting. Be aware of the noises in the room. Slowly open your eyes and then get into a seated position.

After a few minutes, describe, in detail, the house you explored. You can do this to yourself or to another person or a group of people if available.

Next, describe that house again, and this time don't speak for yourself. Speak for the house and its contents. Through you, the house and its contents are describing themselves in the first person. So if the original story contained the words "It was an old house with many things thrown about," the new version would be "I am old and full of disorderly stuff." You must stay in the role of inanimate objects talking in the first person.

Often what happens is quite revealing. In speaking for the house and its possessions, you are describing yourself. You have in fact projected many of your characteristics onto the house and its objects. This is an excellent way to look at yourself; because you do it so indirectly, it is nonthreatening. It produces

candid insights that might otherwise not be available from examination of one's own self-image.

CHANGING YOUR SELF-IMAGE

Another exercise that can have a strong mind-altering effect is
using your awareness to get a new perspective on your problems
and your life. To do this exercise, think of an issue in your life
that you would be willing to be rid of. Start by asking yourself
if you are really willing to be rid of it. Are you willing to have it
vanish from your life right now? This is harder than we think.
It turns out that we love to hang on to some of our issues. We
use them to identify who we are, and to relate through them to
our friends. For instance, some of us *like* to be seen as victims
because people will show us sympathy.

Assuming you find something you are truly willing to be rid
of, the rest is easy. It is simply a matter of being mindful about
all the things you associate with this issue. Being mindful, in
general, implies being aware of what you are doing and not
being on automatic pilot as you go through your day. There is a
bit more to it, however.

True mindfulness is seeing without judging. It is the equivalent of just being there and dispassionately observing what is
going on and what we are doing. It is a state of being willing
to just *be* with whatever is going on. To get to that state, it
helps to pause for a moment, breathe, connect with your inner
experience, and observe the world around you. Mindfulness
can lead to insights and awareness.

YOUR TURN

In the 1970s I participated in a two-weekend workshop known
as Erhard Seminar Training (usually abbreviated in lowercase

as est). On the second day the group was led through an exercise called the Truth Process. I found, to my surprise, that the exercise completely eliminated an annoying habit of speech that I had picked up years earlier. I was naturally impressed, and I incorporated the exercise into my teaching. The results have been very favorable. It is a good tool for getting rid of aspects of your self-image that stand in the way of developing your achievement habit.

Over time, my version of this exercise has changed. I do not run it with a written script, and each year it comes out of my mouth a bit differently. I do not think there is any critical exactness to it. The same ideas have been applied in many versions long before my first experience with the Truth Process.[4]

In this exercise you become mindful of as many things as possible associated with a specific issue. It will work best to lie down in a quiet place and close your eyes. If you are doing this in a group, someone can lead you through it. If not, you can record the instruction and lead yourself. Once you are settled, do a short meditation to relax yourself. A good way to do this is to become aware of your breath and notice the temperature of the air going in and coming out. Then, move your awareness slowly around your body. (The meditation script given above for guided fantasy works nicely.)

After the relaxation, think of an issue that you are willing to be rid of. The issue can have to do with a relationship in your personal or professional life, a mannerism you have, or a decision you are troubled about. It can be anything that has an impact on you on a personal level. It should not be something global like world peace or saving the planet, unless those are personal parts of a problem that you are actually dealing with.

Once you have an issue you are willing to have disappear

from your life, you can proceed to work through the steps in the next paragraphs. If at any time during this exercise you feel that you have rid yourself of whatever you wanted to be rid of, you can move directly to the last two steps in the exercise.

STEPS IN THIS EXERCISE

- First, in your mind's eye, create an object that represents your issue—that is, give the issue an actual physical embodiment. Imagine this object being a few feet in front of you. With your eyes closed, *look* at this embodiment. Become mindful of its physical properties by doing an inventory using the following questions: How tall is it? How wide is it? How deep is it? What is its color? What is its texture? What is its temperature? Does it have an odor? What is its sound?
- Now recall the last time this issue occurred in your life. Then recall the previous time, and keep going back in time until you come as close as possible to the first time it occurred.
- When you are finished, again imagine that your issue's physical embodiment is a few feet in front of you, and repeat the inventory of its physical properties. (Usually the object's properties will have changed slightly.)
- Now recall all the things that you are *sure* are correct about this issue. Don't lie to yourself.
- When you are finished, imagine yet again that the object's physical embodiment is a few feet in front of you, and repeat the inventory of its physical properties. (Note: Repeat this survey of the object's properties after each of the following items.)

- Next, tell yourself all the things you think *might* be correct about this issue.
- Now look at all the things you think might be *incorrect* about this issue.
- Now recall all the things that happen to your body when you experience this issue.
- What are your body positions when this issue comes up for you?
- Do you have any physical reactions associated with this issue?
- Now recall all the emotional states you go through when you have this experience. Think back to the actual experience—not your ideas about it!
- Now look at all the sensations and feelings you associate with this issue. Don't lie to yourself.
- Next, look at all the evaluations and judgments you have regarding this issue.
- Now tell yourself all the things you get out of keeping this issue in your life. Don't lie to yourself. What does it do for you to keep this issue?
- Now imagine being upset about this issue. Next, imagine not being upset about this issue. Again imagine being upset and then not being upset, and repeat about five times. Then imagine having an upset about this issue. Next, imagine not having an upset about this issue. Again imagine having an upset and not having an upset, repeating about five times. Next, imagine being upset and then not being upset, and then having an upset and not having an upset.
- Now imagine you are in front of a whiteboard mounted on a frame with wheels. On this whiteboard write a list of all the things, and people's names, that are keeping this issue

in your life. At this point again imagine that the object's physical embodiment is a few feet in front of you, and repeat the inventory of its physical properties for the last time.

- Now imagine you are again in front of the whiteboard and that you have an eraser in your hand. Look over your list of what is keeping this problem in your life. Erase all things or people's names that are no longer valid. Now imagine pushing the whiteboard up to the edge of a high precipice that has a seemingly bottomless drop on the other side.

- Take one last look at your list, erase anything else you want from it, and then push the board over the precipice.

- Now imagine yourself at the beach on a nice, sunny day. Do your favorite thing for a while. When you feel ready, open your eyes and slowly get up.

- Take all the time you need to quietly digest what you went through during this exercise.

PARTING LESSONS FROM FRIENDS

I have always felt affection for the Welsh and Irish poets and playwrights. Dylan Thomas's poem "Do Not Go Gentle into That Good Night" has always resonated with me, and earlier in my life I thought of myself going to the grave kicking and screaming. Unfortunately I have had too much contact with death to remain guided by my youthful emotions. What I have found is that deaths, like lives, are unique, and that if I pay attention, each death provides me some wisdom.

Karel Deleeuw's death was a celebrated murder case. Karel was a mathematics professor and a close friend who lived on the same street as I on the Stanford campus; we were frequent visitors to each other's homes. Two nights before Ruth and I left on a trip, Karel and I were amusing ourselves reading bizarre ads in a Berkeley newspaper. One ad was for an audiotape that explained how to return from the dead; it came with a T-shirt. The ad's irresistible appeal was its statement, "Buy this shirt and tape, who wants to be dead forever?" So we sent away for the shirt and the tape.

When Ruth and I returned from our trip, we were surprised to find Karel's wife, Sita, at the San Francisco airport to meet us. She was wearing the T-shirt Karel and I had ordered. I started to joke about the shirt when she stopped me to tell us that Karel had been murdered, bludgeoned to death by Ted Streleski, a longtime PhD candidate in Stanford's Department of Mathematics.

Streleski felt he had not been treated fairly by the department, and he wanted to bring public attention to his case. Even though his advisor had recently told him that his work was acceptable for submission as a PhD dissertation, and graduation was finally in sight, he felt his life had been ruined by the long delay in obtaining his degree. Many mathematicians had done their best work when they were young, and now he felt he was too old to become great.

He was stuck in the wrongheaded view of achievement that says accolades and awards are the most important things in life. He had brainwashed himself into thinking that this was all that mattered. And because of this, he was more interested in his grievance than in his degree. He considered the standard avenues of redress, such as writing letters to newspapers, Stanford administrators, or Stanford alumni, or filing an official grievance. He decided these would not be strong enough. He concluded that he could get much greater publicity if he murdered someone prominent and then went to trial.

He made a "hit list" of several professors in the mathematics department and then used public transportation from his apartment in San Francisco to Stanford in an incredibly circuitous route. When he finally got to Stanford, he was unable to find the first few people on his list. Then he got to Karel's name, and unfortunately Karel was in his office, grading the final exams from his summer class. Streleski had brought a small sledgehammer and used it to murder Karel. He then left undetected. A few days later he surrendered to the police.

His idea was to plead not guilty and have a trial that would be covered by the press. During his trial he planned to have members of the mathematics department faculty on the witness stand and question them so as to publicly reveal practices that he felt were abusive.

He succeeded, to a certain degree; he got publicity, and there was some linking of his case to the general plight of PhD students as a political underclass. This incident was a prime example, to me, of the weakness of pure logic. Streleski's logic was impeccable in terms of his desire to get the most publicity for his case, except he forgot the commandment "Thou shalt not kill." Unfortunately, this kind of omission is much too prevalent in decision making at various levels of our society. Streleski was just another tragic example.

I went to the trial every day. Streleski pleaded not guilty, even though he admitted committing the murder as well as having planned to do it, using the sledgehammer he brought with him. His lawyer wanted him to plead not guilty by reason of insanity; Streleski refused because he did not want to be regarded as insane. He wanted to convince the media that the murder was "logically and morally correct" and that it was "a political statement" about the department's treatment of its graduate students.

Here was a bright man who could have had a good life had he not been so fixated on what he felt was "owed" him. If he couldn't have his perfectly planned life as a math genius, then he would make people pay. In doing so, of course, he made himself miserable too. There is no degree, award, job, or referral worth dying or killing for. Of course, most people are not murderers, and this is an extreme case, yet it highlights the danger of being too rigid in your view of what your life path should be. Life will throw you curveballs; if you adapt, you can find happiness in any situation.

My close colleague Rolf Faste's death was remarkable in that he did not follow the expected knee-jerk reaction of seeking survival at any price. To be a traditional "achiever," you're supposed to fight, fight, fight for your life! Rolf didn't really care about what others thought, however. His achievements would be on his own terms. After he was diagnosed with stomach cancer, he noticed that when he visited his regular doctor, the experience left him feeling bad. When he went to his Zen master, he came home feeling good.

He resolved to treat his body as a sacred gift and not to poison it in the name of survival. He made it clear he did not welcome visitors advising him to seek standard chemotherapy or radiation treatments. He spent his time quietly meditating and in positive conversations with family and friends. He died according to the same principles he had lived by.

By contrast, another colleague, who was a difficult person, totally changed while undergoing hospice care. He was not someone I was close to. We had a cordial relationship, even though I did not enjoy his company. After he got sick, I went to visit him at home out of obligation. To my surprise he had changed and was now engaging to be with. I ended up visiting him frequently.

Other colleagues started coming regularly to visit. We all found him to now be a very attractive companion. Finally, close to death, he had stopped posturing and was simply there with us. It was a pity he had to be dying before he felt free to be at ease with his true self. He and everyone around him would have had a better life if he had arrived there sooner.

Bill Moggridge was a close friend who had a strong sense of self and was extremely independent. Nobody could get him to wear a bicycle helmet, even when we came roaring down the mountain passing cars on blind turns. When he asked himself the question "Who are you?" that's what he came up with. He decided how he wanted to live his life and didn't let anyone interfere.

When he became ill, he adapted the same inner strength toward the invasive treatments. His positive attitude gave him a remarkable ability to maintain a normal work life in conditions where most others would simply shut down.

Finally, when it was clear he was dying, he made it easy to be open about his situation. The first morning I walked into his hospital room, he asked me if I had been at the bedside of many dying friends. I knew he was telling me it was okay to be open in talking to him about his condition. It was an extremely generous gift.

Bill was hospitalized in a substandard situation in New York. There he became accepting of various abusive and neglectful practices. I was surprised at how accepting he was. Then I realized it was protective behavior. He was "going along in order to get along." He probably figured if he was no trouble, he would get as good care as they were capable of providing. Finally his care conditions got so bad that it was decided to move him from New York to a hospice facility in San Francisco.

The move required an overnight stay in a motel near the San Francisco airport. The next morning five of us were involved in moving Bill from the motel room to a waiting station wagon. He could not walk, so we moved him in a chair from the motel room to the door of the station wagon. Because he was a big guy, it was not clear how best to maneuver him onto the front seat.

His two sons, Eric and Alex, Izzy (a friend from New York), Matt (Bill's trusted colleague from work), and I were discussing different ways to proceed. Unfortunately, it was cold due to raw summer fog and chilling wind. The discussion went on too long. Finally Bill had had enough. He had said almost nothing in the past day, and when he had spoken, it was very soft and hard to understand. Now, in a booming voice, he said, "Bernie, you shut up. Izzy, you shut up. Eric, you shut up, Alex, you shut up. Matt, you decide!"

It was a magic moment: my friend Bill had come alive, and he was expressing his own self-image to us. He was a problem solver till the end and had taken charge of the situation. With his British accent, it was as though Dylan Thomas himself was telling us he would not be going gently into that good night. That was his great gift to us all.

YOUR TURN

Imagine you have only ten minutes to live. What would you do?
Imagine you have only ten days to live. What would you do?
Imagine you have only ten months to live. What would you do?
Imagine you have only ten years to live. What would you do?

Imagine you have only the rest of your life to live. What would you do?

Looking at your answers to these questions, you have a lot of information about yourself. In this exercise we are talking about your endgame. Can you think of any changes you would like to design into your self-image? Start designing and changing! None of the friends I just told you about knew when they would enter the final countdown. I don't know when mine will come, and you don't know yours either. One thing for sure—it is closer today than it was yesterday, and it will be closer still tomorrow. So now is the time to develop into the person you want to be.

POINT OF VIEW REVISITED

Story writers are concerned with different points of view. They classify them as an objective point of view, a third-person point of view, a first-person point of view, an omniscient point of view, and a limited omniscient point of view.

In the objective point of view the writer takes the position of a detached observer, never telling more than can be directly inferred from the dialogue and action. In the third-person point of view the narrator does not participate in the action of the story; we find out about the characters through the narrator's outside voice.

In the first-person point of view the narrator is a participant in the story, and now the trustworthiness of the account is in question because it might lack objectivity. In omniscient accounts the writer knows everything about all the characters and actions or, in a more limited version, knows everything about a limited number of characters or actions.

In real life, we get to write our own stories. Some people

may be arrogant enough to think they can take on an objective or omniscient point of view, and some rare people might be disassociated enough from their lives to take on a third-person point of view. Some people have the delusion they can take on *any* point of view. Perhaps they can for brief moments, but most of us are all limited to a first-person point of view, and just as in fiction, the question of reliability arises.

Because we are *writing* our own life stories in the first person, we need to realize that we give ourselves and all the other characters their meaning.

THERE ARE MANY FACTORS at play in determining your self-image, and you can shape and redesign that image at will whenever it doesn't suit you. Whether that includes physical things like getting a haircut or losing weight, personality-based things such as correcting bad habits or improving skills, or changing pieces of your identity outright (like changing a name), it's important to know that your self-image doesn't have to stay stagnant. If you've defined yourself as lazy, a bad speller, messy, easily distracted, or selfish, that doesn't have to be an eternal part of your self-concept. You can make a decision right now to see yourself differently, and then to become different.

the
BIG
PICTURE

CHAPTER 9

Insanity in individuals is something rare—but in groups,
parties, nations, and epochs it is the rule.
—*Friedrich Nietzsche*

Life on every level is full of complexity and uncertainty. As individuals we face a life of unknown duration, during which we are likely to go through periods of family, career, or personal crisis. The world around us is even more unpredictable. I am always amazed that things work as well as they do.

It's a very good idea to have a general sense of your goals in life, and an equally good idea not to get too rigid about your path. Stay open to possibility: let other people in, and listen when new opportunities present themselves.

LIFE AS CHANCE

My life seems to have been punctuated by a set of unforeseen detours, followed by surprising right and left turns—anything other than a series of planned, rational steps. This puts me in a difficult situation when students ask for career advice.

I attempt to give it my best shot, which is a rational, linear extrapolation from the present to the future, though I know that the chance of what I say ever becoming reality is very slight. I sometimes tell students, "Life is an adventure, so loosen up, stop trying to figure it out, and just go with the flow." This does not seem to satisfy most of them, so I play the sage, knowing full well their lives will soon deviate from any rational life path that they may have laid out.

I do not have the time or audacity to tell the students how I ended up living and teaching at Stanford, but I will tell you here.

My wife and I both grew up in the same New York City neighborhood near Bronx Park. Despite my inauspicious start as a lazy high school student who spent his time on the streets, I went on to college locally, where I nearly flunked out. The wake-up call I needed was the letter from the dean telling me that I was on academic probation.

Wait, they can't flunk me out! I thought. I knew I wasn't stupid.

From then on, I was a straight-A student. I learned to love school, and I wanted to continue, so I went on to graduate school. As a grad student I also began lecturing at City College, and teaching spoke to me. I really enjoyed it. As I was nearing the completion of my PhD studies at Columbia University, I had a discussion with my thesis advisor about my future. To my absolute delight, he suggested I apply to join the Columbia faculty. He cautioned me that it would be prudent to also apply elsewhere, because there was at the time some pushback about inbreeding in the mechanical engineering department.

He mentioned that Cornell University was looking for a young assistant professor. I, in turn, recalled that several years back I had spent a summer in Los Angeles and heard that the area around Stanford University was a nice place to live. I asked if my thesis advisor knew anyone on the Stanford faculty. Yes, he knew a Professor Arnold. Herein lies the tale of coincidences that got me to Stanford, where I have spent well over fifty years of my life.

The International Conference for Teachers of Mechanisms was held at Yale University in March 1961, under the auspices of the National Science Foundation. The organizers of the conference mailed an invitation to Professor Arnold at Stanford University.

At Stanford's Department of Mechanical Engineering there were two people with the last name Arnold. John E. Arnold was a famous professor in both mechanical engineering and the business school; he was the founding head of the department's Design Division. Frank A. Arnold, on the other hand, was a lecturer associated with the Thermosciences Division, who was interested in the aerodynamics of flight—not mechanisms. The conference invitation mistakenly went to Frank rather than John. Not deterred by this obvious error, Frank accepted the invitation and attended the conference, where he met my thesis advisor.

Thus when my advisor wrote about me to his acquaintance, he was writing to the wrong person. Happily, this time Frank passed the letter on to John. My advisor had a very strong reputation, and based on that, John Arnold invited me to come to Stanford for an interview.

Meanwhile, I had received an offer letter from Columbia University. I had accepted the position of assistant professor, and was to start that September. I was looking forward to teaching at Columbia, working closely with my thesis advisor. I was nevertheless glad to be offered a free interview trip to California. In late July my wife and I arranged for a nanny to watch our two young boys and my twelve-year-old sister, who lived with us, and we boarded a train for California.

At Stanford I was very impressed with John Arnold. I learned he had been a popular professor at MIT and had only been at Stanford a few years. The Design Division he had created was composed of three young faculty members at the beginning of their careers, and the atmosphere was very different from what I was used to at Columbia. John had a special slant on education and engineering that was influenced by his having studied philosophy before going into engineering. Most of all, I noticed a special twinkle in his eye that made me feel that it would be interesting to work with him.

I was thus pleased when, after a half day of interviews and a lunch meeting, the chairman of the department told me they would be recommending me for a three-year tenure-track assistant professor appointment. That evening the concern set in. My wife was very attracted to the area, and John Arnold and the job seemed appealing; however, I really liked New York, my thesis advisor, and Columbia. Besides, Columbia University was starting the fall semester in a month, and I had already accepted the appointment. What to do?

If I did move to Stanford, I would be arriving in a month with a family and no place to stay. I put down a deposit for a house rental, knowing full well that the odds were I would forfeit the deposit and end up staying in New York. My wife and I agonized over this decision during the long train ride across the country back to New York.

When I arrived back at Columbia, my thesis advisor asked what had happened, and I told him I had been offered the job. Without hesitation he told me he had been discussing that possibility with his colleagues, and that they had heard that Stanford was going through a large building up of faculty. They believed Stanford was headed toward a new era, and felt it would be in my best interest to accept the offer. Furthermore, I should not be concerned about my last-minute reneging at Columbia. In an instant the problem with Columbia was resolved. That only left the task of informing our families that we were leaving and taking the children three thousand miles away. And, yes, my twelve-year-old sister was horrified at the prospect of having to leave her girlfriends.

I have had a long and satisfying career at Stanford, and it took a host of improbable events for me to get here in the first place. My life is punctuated by milestones that would have never happened except for the combination of unplanned and improbable chance events.

Most people I know have similarly nonlinear life trajectories. How about you? Have you had enough unexpected developments in your life to sign on to the life-is-a-chance theory? If yes, learn to enjoy the trip and don't waste your cross-country train ride worrying about what to decide.

OPPORTUNITIES

Some people almost never need to make agonizing decisions; life for them just seems to flow along, and when the big transitions happen, they notice they were big only in hindsight. I am one of those people; I consider myself lucky to have had that type of a career. And thinking about the many crossroads in a long and full career, I now see that if I had not responded to certain opportunities, my life would have been quite different. I will never know, of course, what might have been. Still, I have no regrets.

There are two extreme types of people in the world—those who say yes to every opportunity, and those who say no. I place myself in the middle.

I have found it is important to be mindful of my reactions to opportunities. There is no way to know in advance where these will lead. Some may lead nowhere, and some to disaster. Yet when opportunity presents itself, we have no choice but to respond. (Ignoring opportunity is itself a response.)

Several life-changing opportunities have come to me in the form of out-of-the-blue phone calls. The first came in my second year at Stanford. I answered my office phone and was asked to hold: Dr. Terman wanted to talk. Of course I knew the name—Fredrick Terman was Stanford's provost, a legendary electrical engineer who had been the mentor of Bill Hewlett and David Packard—however, I had never met him. What could he possibly want with a young assistant professor?

Terman informed me that he was calling to suggest that I provide some expertise in the design of machines to John McCarthy, a mathematician who had just won a large government grant to found the Stanford Artificial Intelligence Laboratory. Part of the grant was to go toward the development of robotic devices. Terman had been told that John was too mathematical to handle the design of actual devices, and that I could provide necessary engineering skills.

Terman's phone call led to my close collaboration with the Stanford Artificial Intelligence Laboratory and my immersion in robotics, which became a major part of my creative work for over forty years. I became one of the founders in the new field of robotics, and John grew to be a lifelong friend. He was one of the main creators of the field of artificial intelligence, a true genius with an incredibly inquisitive and creative mind. I soon found out he was much more practical than Terman had been led to believe.

John had a charming belief that he could solve any problem.

In the early days I traveled with him to Houston, where the two of us met with oil-company executives in a fancy conference room near the top of a large skyscraper. John was trying to convince them to fund the development of a robotic coal-mining machine. We had never done anything remotely like that, but John described in detail what he imagined such an undertaking would accomplish. He showed a film our students had made of a robot arm assembling a tower of blocks. The background music on the film was Scott Joplin's ragtime melody "The Entertainer," which had been used in the film *The Sting*. In the film, two hustlers (played by Paul Newman and Robert Redford) con a mob boss out of a lot of money. As I sat there, I realized John was not aware of the strong parallel between our fanciful request and *The Sting*'s plot. We never got the money. To this day I am sure the oil men saw the irony and had a good laugh.

I remember that my initial reaction to Terman's phone call was at best neutral. At first I felt that the opportunity presented was a distraction from my main research. However, it turned out I was able to bring my unique perspective to what John was doing, and the robotics work in turn enhanced my main area of interest, kinematics.

Another phone call that changed my life was from my friend Mike Rabins, a professor at Texas A&M University, who wanted to know if I'd organize a summer creativity workshop. My immediate reaction was an emphatic *"No way,"* but just as I was about to hang up, I realized it could be a good opportunity for my friend Rolf Faste to build up his reputation and get promoted. He and I wound up leading these workshops for ten years.

The opportunity I reluctantly accepted—for reasons that never materialized (Rolf never applied for the promotion)—ended up having a major impact on me. Teaching methodology and experience-based learning became a big part of my life, and I had a new basis for interacting with colleagues throughout the world.

These two big changes in my career were instigated by phone calls that I had no idea were coming. I immediately accepted the life changes offered in the phone calls. In retrospect I had no idea how large a change was to come. Each started out as just another everyday occurrence. There were no agonizing decisions, no long-term life plans—nothing other than the ordinary flow of my life. I was not looking for change, and would probably have had a fulfilling and rich life without those changes; happily they were more than satisfying.

Looking back and thinking about those phone calls, I realize that I could have just as easily said no to both of them, and in so doing missed two of the most gratifying developments in my professional life. Life is full of junctures and opportunities, and it is impossible to know in advance which way to go, and which chances to take. I feel very lucky that I said yes to these opportunities.

THE BLESSING OF WORK

Much has been written about automation and the replacement of human workers with machines. Two main justifications are usually given for mechanizing jobs once done by humans: first, that the work is tedious and dangerous, so it's better to let machines do it for the workers' sake; and second, that workers are expensive and unreliable, so machines can save money while retaining or improving quality.

These ideas are basically derived from the context of

blue-collar factory work. They do little to address the computer revolution and the great changes that have occurred across the workforce, replacing a large number of highly trained and educated scientific and technical workers with machines. This trend toward more and more automation brings into play the question of what meaning we give to work.

The current situation was in some ways anticipated by writers from as far back as the earliest days of the Industrial Revolution. One of the most prescient books in this genre was written by Kurt Vonnegut right after World War II. In *Player Piano* he describes a future America where the majority of the people are either unemployed or working in highly alienating jobs, in a desultory army or doing meaningless public works projects.[1] These people live across a river—it could just as well be the other side of the tracks or highway—from a small educated elite that runs the economy. In this society, machines do most of the work, and the jobs left for the majority of the human population provide no satisfaction.

A more nuanced understanding of the changes brought about by the way people choose to develop technology can be found in Harry Braverman's scholarly treatise *Labor and Monopoly Capital*. Braverman points out that work that allows for self-expression satisfies human needs, and he traces the roots of the trend toward deskilling of both work and workers. In Braverman's terms, the machines that enhance people's skills are considered *life-supporting*, while those that deskill people and devalue their work are *life-destroying*.[2]

Perhaps the best spokesperson for the need to define the proper role of machines is Mahatma Gandhi. Asked whether he was opposed to machines, he answered,[3]

How can I be when I know that even this body is a most delicate piece of machinery? The spinning wheel is a machine, a little toothpick is a machine. What I object to is the craze for machinery, not machinery as such. The craze is for what they call labour-saving machinery. Men go on "saving labour" till thousands are without work and thrown on the open streets to die of starvation. I want to save time and labour, not for a fraction of mankind but for all. I want the concentration of wealth, not in the hands of a few, but in the hands of all. Today machinery merely helps a few to ride on the backs of millions.

The issues raised by Braverman and Gandhi are eloquently reinforced by E. F. Schumacher,[4] who looks at work from a Buddhist point of view. In his classic essay "Buddhist Economics," Schumacher points out that work serves to feed our basic need for association with other people. In fact, work supplies several of our basic human needs:[5]

1. It gives people a chance to utilize and develop their faculties.
2. It enables people to overcome their ego-centeredness by joining with others in a common task.
3. It brings forth the goods and services for a becoming existence.

With this in mind, Schumacher points out that work is a basic human function that transcends the usual economic meanings associated with it:

To organize work in such a manner that it becomes meaningless, boring, stultifying, or nerve wracking for the worker would be little short of criminal; it would indicate a greater concern with goods than with people, an evil lack of compassion and a soul-destroying degree of attachment to the most primitive side of this worldly existence. Equally, to strive for leisure as an alternative to work would be a complete misunderstanding of one of the basic truths of human existence, namely that work and leisure are complementary parts of the same living process and cannot be separated without destroying the joy of work and the bliss of leisure.

If I am inspired by the humanity and beauty of Schumacher's description of the Buddhist conception of what is called right livelihood, where does that leave me in terms of the current conditions in my own society? The answer, for me, comes from a strange place. I found it in Lawrence Weschler's book *Seeing Is Forgetting the Name of the Thing One Sees*, an examination of the life and work of the contemporary artist Robert Irwin.[6]

What is unusual and inspiring about Irwin is the experimentation he brought to exploring the boundaries of his craft. To me Irwin's journey is a model for anyone in any walk of life. Take control over your life and work, it tells us. Instead of following the normal course of his profession, Irwin followed his curiosity and created a unique path of exploration and wonderment that provided a life force based on self-expression.

At least two things happen to most students who read Irwin's biography. First, and most important, they realize that they do not need to stay within the bounds of their profession as taught in school or practiced by their peers. Second, they learn about perception, which is for most of them a useful new way of seeing the world. As the title says, "Seeing is forgetting the name of the thing one sees."

Even those who stay in the system can make meaningful choices that support their principles and set them apart from their professional colleagues. Some people, for example—myself included—do not, as a matter of principle, do military work. Others choose to work on social betterment projects. More telling than the choice of work is an individual's attitude toward and relationship to his work. Many people associate the freedom to make such choices only with highly skilled professional work. My experience is that such choices are available even in the most seemingly menial jobs.

I worked my way through school with various jobs. I have worked as a gas station attendant, a riveter, a handyman, a warehouse hauler, a door-to-door salesman, a stock clerk, a deliveryman, a street vendor, a postal clerk, a chicken farmer, an engineer, and a teacher. Was I any less intelligent or less of a person when I didn't have a PhD attached to my name? No matter what work any of us does or what background we come from, we get to decide how to see ourselves and our world.[7] When you hold yourself in high esteem and keep a positive outlook on your future, others usually follow suit. By choosing the meaning we give to the people and things in our environment, ultimately we control our own experiences, no matter what work we are doing.

FULFILLING OTHERS' EXPECTATIONS

One of the hardest things can be to follow a path that's different from what your family or society expects of you. It's very possible that you were expected to join the family business, or have the same career and life trajectory as your parents. And maybe that would make you happy—and maybe it wouldn't.

When I grew up in the Bronx, my friend Mark got a lot of pressure from his parents because he was not paying attention to his schoolwork; he spent all of his time on the street, fixing cars. They insisted he go to a counselor, who put him through a battery of tests. The results showed that he had an aptitude for doing things with his hands! He ended up moving to a small town, where he opened a printing business and lived happily ever after.

Like Mark, many of us do have a sense as to what kinds of things we are good at and what naturally appeals to us, yet we are surrounded by well-meaning people like Mark's parents who have formed ideas about what is the best path for us. The two idea streams are often in conflict.

When my wife, Ruth, was in school, her parents insisted that she study something marketable like secretarial or teaching skills, instead of doing the artistic and creative problem-solving work she was born for. This pressure led to a wrong professional choice, and it took many years for her to get on the proper path.

Sometimes, though, you can be lucky and have a protector. Andy was my closest friend in graduate school. During his funeral, in a very moving eulogy, his nephew tearfully expressed his gratitude. The nephew, now a successful architect, felt deeply indebted to Andy for having taken him in and supported his studies in architecture after his own father disowned him for deciding not to go into the family business.

Mark, Ruth, and Andy's nephew all faced conflicts about career-path choices. Such issues are very common for college-age students. Even without outside constraints, it is not uncommon for people to change their choices in midstream. Some do it several times. Others spend most of their working lives hunting for the right career, and some drop out completely. Often when I speak with students, I explain to them that many people, even very successful ones, do not know what they will do "when they grow up." It is all part of the adventure of life, and the best thing is to enjoy the voyage.

The constraints on our career paths tend to be self-imposed. It is said that we all rise to our level of incompetence. I can't say that I have found much truth in that. What I find more to be the case is that we tend to *rise without thinking*. There is a ladder that exists in many career paths, and society brainwashes people to think they are supposed to climb it. Not every new award, degree, or promotion is a good thing for the individual.

There are a great many ex-somethings floating around who would have led much more satisfying and productive lives if they had stayed in the trenches, doing what they really enjoyed, rather than moving in what looked like an upward direction. A woman named Diane spent many years as a nurse before getting promoted to supervisor and then to administrator. It was a lot more money and power, yet she realized that she wasn't helping anybody anymore, and quit. Being so far removed from the patients she cared about had killed her enthusiasm for the job. Now she's a martial arts instructor instead!

If in doubt, go back to the earlier exercise where you asked yourself three questions: "Who am I?" "What do I want?" "What is my purpose?"

It's a good idea to revisit that exercise frequently. Now I'd like you to do it once more and add a new word: "What do I *really* want?" Keep asking it, over and over, until you feel you have gained insight into your own desires so you're no longer at the mercy of society's ideas of what is good for you.

WHAT WE TAKE FOR GRANTED

The most important things we can know about a man are the things he takes for granted, and the most important things to know about a society are those which are simply assumed and seldom noticed.[8]
—*Lewis Wirth*

The things we take for granted, and simply assume, are the basis for our self-image, and give the things in our lives their meaning. By making our background assumptions explicit, we are able to affirm them or change them. Doing this gives us the opportunity to change ourselves from puppets to truly autonomous beings.

Some people achieve autonomy through sheer stubbornness and rebelliousness. Although that may work, it is not a healthy way to approach change. A more rational approach is to look at everything that is obvious to you.

YOUR TURN

Make a list of all the things in your life that you do not normally notice. A good heading for such a list is "Things that are too obvious or too trivial to list."

For example, your list might include the following:

I don't really listen when my wife talks to me.
I will never clean out the garage.
I do not get enough sleep.
I never seem to get around to phoning my cousin.
I always support the same political party that my parents did.
My attitude toward money is the same as my father's.

In the coming days, notice how much of your behavior is based on items on this list. If you are happy with these things, go on with your life. If you want to change any of them, cross them out on the list—both actually and metaphorically.

One of the things I very much like about problem statements in the form of points of view (see chapter 3) is that the POV statement tends to reveal underlying assumptions and make the desired objectives explicit. Formerly, many people operated on the basis of unspoken and unnoticed assumptions. Now, with POV, more assumptions are stated explicitly. Unfortunately, countless assumptions still go unnoticed and may in fact unnecessarily bias the solution.

The role unquestioned assumptions play becomes obvious if we look back at sociopolitical norms of the past, things like the absolute power of royalty, political participation only for men, property passed to the eldest son, slavery, serfdom, a prohibition on divorce, only men being allowed to file for divorce, only property holders being allowed to vote, child labor, colonization, and the "white man's burden." For a long time each of these was assumed to be an intrinsic part of the given culture, and passed unnoticed and uncontested until its presence was brought into the foreground and its legitimacy questioned.

A parable that nicely illustrates the relativistic nature of our social norms is the story of the young man who walked into a small town dressed only in a white sheet and did not speak except for babbling sounds. The townspeople assumed the poor fellow was insane and locked him up in their mental hospital. A week later, twenty more people walked into town, dressed identically in white sheets and babbling in the same way as the original fellow. At this point the townspeople released the first man; clearly he was part of a religious sect.

The overriding message here is that if you are going to do

something outlandish, you had better get a group together; otherwise, people will think you are crazy.

Many institutions in our society are widely accepted, and yet if you looked at them within the white-sheet-babbling framework, they would make no sense if there weren't a lot of people participating in them. Imagine what would happen if there were no universities, and I approached you on the street and suggested that you pay me a lot of money for at least four years. In return I would give you lectures on subjects you have never heard of that I happen to be interested in, and if you jumped through enough hoops, at the end of the four years I would give you a piece of paper with your name on it—let's call it a BS. Would that sound reasonable?

I once heard an Indian guru give a parable describing the history of banking.

A man was sitting on his front porch, watching the world go by, when suddenly he got a vision consisting of four letters: B-A-N-K. So he got a piece of chalk and wrote the letters on his front door. Shortly thereafter someone came up to him and gave him some money. The man was surprised and perplexed, so he put the money in a large box. All day long people kept giving him money, and he kept being perplexed and putting the money into the box. Finally, at the end of the day, the man went into his house and took all his money out from under his mattress and put it in the same box.

The story was told to warn the guru's followers about self-delusion and false prophets. It makes the point that if enough people do it, it stops being crazy and instead becomes the accepted norm. The famous tulip, stock market, dot-com, and housing bubbles are just the tip of the iceberg for this type of me-too behavior. Unfortunately this tendency to relabel the crazy as normal doesn't apply only to financial situations; it is also at the heart of some of the world's greatest political and social conflicts.

In the many ongoing conflicts between people and nations, each side justifies itself by pointing out some wrong done to it by the other side. Each side's story makes perfect sense, and justifies whatever they do in response. The interesting thing that often goes unnoticed is that the justification depends on where they start the story. I call this a question of punctuation, and although it goes unacknowledged by the belligerents, it is of utmost importance.

History is an ongoing flow. For all practical purposes—other than in our individual lives—there is no beginning or end. So all stories that are told with a beginning are distortions of what has happened. Where the story starts colors it so as to justify the storyteller's position. The ongoing slaughter between Muslims and Hindus did not start with who threw the first stone after the Indian subcontinent's partition. The trouble in your marriage did not start when your wife went out with her ex-boyfriend or when your husband did not clean the garage. By deciding where to start the story or where to put the period, you give the story its meaning. By changing the punctuation, you can make the hero into the villain, and vice versa.

The problem is that most of us are too busy seeing all the babbling sheets around us. If that is all we see, it becomes very difficult for us to see that we and our fellows are not acting like autonomous, reasonable, rational beings.

In many ways our self-image is intimately related to what we choose as our identity. We often hold a few items so strongly that we lose our autonomy and in effect become puppets. These items should certainly be on your list of "things that are too obvious or too trivial to list." If you are willing to cut the puppeteer's strings while still holding on to your identity, you might free yourself to rewrite your conflict stories with different punctuation.

SOMETIMES YOU'RE GOING TO SCREW UP

Somewhere along the way, all of us will screw up. Some of us will screw up more than others; it's just plain going to happen.

You'll fudge something on a résumé and get caught. You'll say something insulting about your boss and find out he's within earshot. You'll accept credit for something that was really someone else's idea. You'll sneak into work late and pretend you were there all along.

Here's the thing: Presidents Richard Nixon and Bill Clinton both screwed up, yet what got them into real trouble wasn't the original "sin," it was the lies they told afterward. Had each of them fessed up, their troubles would most likely have blown over much faster. Instead we remember "I am not a crook" and "I did not have sexual relations with that woman" as punch lines.

Lies can snowball. You tell one, and then you have to tell another to back it up. When you feel painted into a corner, there's a good solution: tell the truth. It's uncomfortable, and you may get into trouble, yet it will almost certainly be less trouble than if you compound the issue by lying again.

When you get caught with your hand in the cookie jar, don't cover up—fess up.

SOMETIMES WE CAN GET so caught up in the minutiae of our lives that we forget to step back and see the bigger possibilities out there for us. If you've been following a conservative path, why not take a chance and veer off it for a while? Change your surroundings, agree to a friend's crazy plan, tag along on a cross-country trip. Learn about communities different from your own and figure out where you fit in. Remember that the real "big picture" is this: You don't take anything with you when you die, so you might as well spend your time on Earth experiencing all that you can, rather than stagnating and accumulating.

MAKE

ACHIEVEMENT
your habit

CHAPTER 10

Hardening of the categories leads to art disease.

—*Kenneth Snelson*

I take the view that life is basically a problem-solving activity, and you can learn to make both the process and the result better. My goal with this book has been to give you tools and concepts that you can use to achieve a fuller, more fruitful, more satisfying life.

PROBLEMS ARE GOOD FOR YOU

The word *problem* has negative connotations. It implies there is something wrong that needs fixing. However, if a problem is re-framed as an opportunity to make things in our life better, then it becomes a positive, and problem solving can be recognized as one of our basic life forces.

Some enlightened individuals think of all problems as op-portunities. Still, you do not have to wait for enlightenment to realize the positive influence problems can have in your life; you can just look at your own experience. When I'm working on a problem, it can take over my life. I find it hard to go to sleep, and I wake up early, excited to deal with it.

In his classic nineteenth-century Russian novel, Ivan Goncharov creates the antihero Ilya Ilyitch Oblomov, the ultimate embodiment of a superfluous person. Oblomov is incapable of making a decision or undertaking any significant action. He has no real problems, so he rarely leaves his bed. In fact, he fails to leave his bed for the first 150 pages of the novel. This is a fictitious story that, in its time, was meant to parody the life of idle aristocrats. It represents for me a portrait of what happens in a life without problems. It reaffirms my experience that problems, like satisfying work, are gifts that provide vehicles for the natural development of our life-giving forces.

So what are problems?

I use the word *problem* to describe any situation that we want to change. Usually problems are stated as questions ("How do I get a job?") or statements ("I cannot afford college"). Generally we want to deal with problems in order to effect a positive change in some situation.

Life consists of solving a series of problems. We are nearly all very good at it. We learn by repetition, and to a great extent are not consciously aware of our abilities. Most people dress themselves suitably on a daily basis, make their way to their destinations, and accomplish basic tasks such as feeding themselves. Furthermore, they manage all this within their environmental, cultural, and economic constraints.

In addition to this daily onslaught of success, we also find frustrations and failures. We all have unsolved issues in our lives. There are situations and people that bug us, and there are vexing personal and professional problems. It is often easy to resolve these issues by applying the simple techniques described in chapter 3. I've employed these techniques in my own life and shared them with many groups throughout the world.

If you reframe your problem, many possible options become apparent, and the path to a solution often becomes obvious. Once you have a clear view of what you want to accomplish, there are various ways to work out the details.

PROTOTYPE YOUR WAY TO SUCCESS

A *prototype* is a sample or model created to show or test a concept—something to be learned from. In solving problems, an excellent way to move forward is to incorporate prototyping into your process.

Early in the problem-solving process it is best to think of prototypes as simply trial balloons—ideas or statements sent out to gauge people's reactions to your ideas. Prototypes do not necessarily have to resemble a physical object. They can take any form. They could be conversations, written drafts, short movies, skits, physical embodiments of social or personal problems, or actual physical models of objects. Prototypes can be in any form that gives information. They do not need to *look like* or *work like* the final solution, and they certainly do not need to do both.

In a culture of prototyping, things are always being tried out. The road to a final solution is strewn with ideas that have been prototyped as ways to get information, directions to take, ideas to modify, and ideas to abandon. Prototyping is a great way to show people what you have in mind, so you can elicit their feedback. When the result of prototyping is a physical object, it is usually best that it not be too precious. The term *mock-up* is sometimes used to denote an early-stage nonprecious prototype. I think the term *crap-up* would be a better way to describe the ideal early prototype.

YOUR TURN

The next time you are asked to do something, don't spend too much time thinking. Simply charge ahead. Do this by taking the first idea that comes into your head and make a quick prototype (of the "crap-up" variety). Then think about what you have learned from this. If you are brave enough, try it out on some people and get their thoughts.

In the d.school and our design programs at Stanford, prototyping is a way of life. The same is true for our neighbors, the design consultancy IDEO. Between Stanford and IDEO, I have seen thousands of prototyping examples. Most have been very useful, and some have become iconic. In my "Transformative Design" class, a three-student team was interested in improving the patient experience in Stanford Hospital's emergency room. They were particularly interested in how patients in the waiting room were managed. They arranged to visit the emergency room to do patient observations and interviews. Unfortunately, a day before their visit, permission for their visit was revoked due to issues of patient privacy.

Undeterred, the students thought up a prototype that worked like the emergency-room system. They based their prototype on making the need to urinate analogous to the need for emergency medical treatment. They invited a group of friends and asked them to be sure not to have urinated for several hours. When their friends arrived, they offered them drinks and also denied them access to the bathroom. Eventually the bathroom was opened. However, people wanting to use it had to sit in a special waiting area until they were called.

The order of the call was not according to arrival time in the waiting area; it was according to how much a person had drunk. In the students' analogy, the more people drank, the greater their need for priority medical treatment, and thus those who had drunk the most were given earlier access to the bathroom. This prototype yielded important insights as to how to better inform patients and gain their understanding when they see others taken out of turn while waiting for service in a hospital emergency room.

Prototyping like this gets you past the cerebral what-it-might-be-like stage and into the reality of problem solving.

In another case, designers made a film to show how a proposed children's smartphone application would work. Using the app, kids would touch or flick the screen to animate creatures. The film demonstrated this by using a man in place of the creatures.

Was the film made by recording the actual app on a smartphone? No! The prototype was simply a piece of cardboard in the shape of a phone screen, and there was a real person on the other side. The person would move in response to the user's hand as he pretended to touch the imitation phone screen.

In this way the designers could test and demonstrate various different ideas without the need to actually create the animated figure and the programs to control it. This led to Sesame Street's *Elmo's Monster Maker,* a very successful smartphone app for children.

What is being prototyped in these examples is the basic idea—that is, the concept behind the eventual solutions. They fall under the broad heading of *conceptual prototypes*—as opposed to *functional prototypes*, which are made to test the actual functioning of the solution. Because prototypes can be physical objects, sketches, videos, conversations, or any trial balloon, the bottom line with prototyping is to choose the type that will let you learn the most in the fastest way.

Prototyping has different purposes, depending on where we are in the solution process. Let's divide this process into three stages. In the first stage we use prototyping to *inspire* a good concept (this is often called a *concept prototype*). The second stage is to concretely *evolve* the solution (this is a *feasibility prototype*). The final stage is to *validate* that the solution is actually going to work as expected (this is a *functional prototype*). What I have been talking about is mainly the first stage.

As the solution process proceeds, the approximations to the final solution get more exact, and the prototypes tend to become more like dress rehearsals for the real thing.

Even though we rarely think in these formal terms when dealing with personal issues, these same concepts about prototyping apply to most problems. For every issue you deal with, you need to be inspired to find a solution idea, evolve the details of a solution, and validate that the solution works. In everyday life you may show a draft of a letter to someone or simply ask for advice about something you are thinking of doing. By doing this, you too are prototyping. It may be helpful to keep this in mind when you're facing a project you keep putting off. If you've long had an idea for a screenplay at the back of your mind, or if you want to design a dress, don't get caught up in how you're going to get it just right. That's what causes many people to shut down and never get started. Avoid the desire for perfection right out of the gate. Instead, tell yourself that you're *prototyping* your screenplay or your dress. The final version can come later.

KEEP YOUR FOCUS

In problem solving, as in all facets of life, sometimes things go very wrong. When they do go wrong, we tend not to take responsibility for our part in the malfunction. One common way of avoiding responsibility is to label the missteps as *accidents*.

My main athletic activity is biking. I am extremely fortunate in being able to bike to work every day. I also have a group of friends that I ride with on Sundays, and several times a year we go on extended bike trips. This ritual has gone on for over thirty years, and in that time I have witnessed many bike accidents. Unfortunately I, too, have had my share of spills. Looking back over all the accidents I see that almost all of them have a single root cause: loss of focus. I (or someone) wasn't paying attention.

My two worst bicycle accidents are classic examples. In the first, we had cycled over thirty miles from Stanford University to San Francisco. The plan was to take the train back home. When we got within sight of the train station, I felt the ride was over, and I started thinking about a presentation I was scheduled to make that evening. I was not paying attention to riding. Suddenly my tires got trapped in a trolley track groove, and I fell, sprawling into the middle of a busy intersection. Luckily I did not get hit by any vehicles, although I did get badly bruised and bloodied.

If I had been paying attention, I could easily have steered to cross the rail groove at an angle, as the rest of my group did. After this incident I resolved to always keep my focus on the road when I am biking.

Fast-forward a few years, to my usual Sunday ride. One of the other riders was talking to me about his upcoming trip to India, and we were falling behind the rest of the group. As we ended the conversation, I wanted to recommend a change in his itinerary. Momentarily I was not able to recall the name of "that nice city south of Bangalore." I started pedaling faster to catch up to the group, thinking of India and searching my brain for the name I was forgetting. Suddenly I hit what seemed like a three-foot-high wall. My bike flipped 180 degrees, and I landed on my head and shoulders in the middle of the road. The rider I had been talking to immediately stopped the traffic, and eventually I was taken to the side of the road with a trashed helmet, a dislocated shoulder, and a bleeding head and face. Oh, yes, the name of the city was Mysore—sort of poetic justice, don't you think?

The three-foot wall I thought I'd crashed into was in reality a three-inch-high triangular island to split the traffic at a three-way intersection. I had cycled around that island without incident almost every Sunday for over thirty years. Yup, I had broken my vow to not lose focus.

Keeping focus is important in many parts of your life; even if you do not bicycle, it will keep you safe. I am not just talking about driving cars, skateboarding, Rollerblading, piloting an airplane, running, walking, or other forms of physical activity; this holds for all aspects of life. Just as you give life its meaning, you give all your activities their meaning. In addition to your physical activities, your emotional and intellectual activities also require your focus. If you don't focus on these, you may also hit the three-foot-high wall, even if you have gone past it safely many times before. I cannot call such malfunctions "accidents."

IT'S NOT ABOUT YOU

We tend to inflate our own importance in other people's lives and actions, and this is another cause of things going wrong in problem solving and other aspects of our lives. We need to realize that other people are not concerned about our hairstyle or what we are wearing; they are too busy worrying about themselves to take much notice of us. People are mainly preoccupied with their own careers and problems, not yours. In spite of this, many of us believe we are the principal cause of other people's actions.

A more realistic model is implied by the phrase "It's not about me." I often found that when I thought I was the cause of another person's behavior or mood, it turned out later that their actions had nothing to do with me. Even recently, I needed a reminder of this when I took an overseas trip.

I had signed up to give a series of lectures in Santiago, and then to colead a five-day workshop on a ship off the southern coast of Chile. My wife, Ruth, was not happy to be left alone for two weeks. Although I left feeling a bit uneasy, and our parting was strained, I was not overly concerned about her.

As soon as I got to Chile, I sent her a series of e-mails. After three days with no response, I figured she was probably mad at me. So I phoned, thinking that speaking directly would be the best way to clear things up. She did not answer the phone. I left a voice message asking her to phone me. I repeated this four times. She did not return my calls. I felt sure she was mad at me. I phoned our son Elliot and asked him to call her. She always picks up his calls. When he reported that he, too, could not reach her, I started to get very concerned.

I asked Elliot to contact Ruth's friends. Those he could reach did not know where she was. From a neighbor, he found out that her car was still in the carport. The neighbor went into our house, and everything looked normal, however, there was no sign of Ruth.

It was now a few hours before I was scheduled to fly south

from Santiago to meet the ship. I had to decide whether to cancel the trip and fly home. Finally, at the last minute, Elliot found her. She was ill and had been taken to the hospital by a friend.

Ruth had been sending us e-mails the whole time and wondering why no one was responding. She found out later that she hadn't been sending or receiving e-mails because she had not properly connected to the hospital's Wi-Fi system with her new smartphone.

By the time I came back home, Ruth had returned to good health. She had not been mad at me. If I had remembered the mantra "It's not about me," I could have avoided misunderstandings.

YOUR TURN

The next few times something happens where you think people's actions are related to what you did or did not do, tell yourself "It's not about me." Then note how you feel and, if possible, check how they feel.

MOTIVATION

Motivation is at the heart of problem solving. I once returned to Stanford after spending about a month lecturing in China. I was standing in front of a classroom on the first day of the term, looking at a group of graduate students who were there "shopping" for which classes to take. It was my job to motivate them to sit through ten weeks of lectures in my class. What went through my mind was an item on the questionnaire they would be asked to fill out at the end of the last class: "On a scale of 1 to 5, does the teacher motivate me to do my best work?"

In our system it is up to the teacher to motivate the students. If I do not motivate them, I am not doing a good job. For the first time, it seemed absurd to me that I was supposed to motivate graduate students. During my trip to China, I had experienced people who were highly self-motivated to learn. There was a stark contrast between that experience and what I was seeing in my classroom.

My China trip occurred shortly after the normalization of diplomatic relations between the People's Republic of China and the United States, and there was a great societal thrust in China to learn English. No matter what city I was in, every time I left my hotel there would be people waiting outside wanting to practice English. I was enthralled by their eagerness to learn, and at times ended up sitting in the street correcting pronunciation while several people read aloud to me.

Some years later, when I started participating in the Burning Man festival, I was again struck by the power of self-motivation. I witnessed thousands of people who put in endless hours of labor (and, in some cases, lots of money) to create things that had no commercial value. They were doing it for self-satisfaction and the entertainment of their friends; they thought what they were making was cool and they were proud to show it off. Again I thought about this in contrast to my experience as a teacher.

Education systems tend to use rewards as motivators. The most immediate reward is a grade. Once you get a certain number of those, you earn the system's ultimate reward—a degree. The problem with this is that the rewards are basically extrinsic, not intrinsic. Getting a degree for many students is highly instrumental. It is, for them, the same as if they were working all week at an odious job just to earn enough money to have fun on the weekend. The system does not give them the tools to be self-motivated. It may provide heroic role models, but, unfortunately, for most students these models represent an unattainable lifestyle that they can only worship from afar. No matter how high their grades, their education can leave them with a lack of focus, a lack of direction, and a lack of confidence. Many people who graduate are not sure they can do anything. The system is not geared toward fostering their growth to a point where they can develop intrinsic motivation. It often does not give them an opportunity to do something that matters to them and that they feel is actually important.

I have found that project-based learning greatly increases intrinsic motivation. My experience with student motivation comes mainly from my experience at an elite university. In the years when we used to do the two-week creativity workshops, we would often hear, "Well, you can do that at Stanford, but you don't know how impossible that would be back at my school." After the first year, we found a way to answer that concern. Toward the end of the first week we screened a movie called *Stand and Deliver*, based on the true story of a high school math teacher, Jaime Escalante. It shows how he succeeded in getting remarkable results by motivating underperforming, economically challenged students at Garfield High, a high school in the predominantly Hispanic ghetto of East Los Angeles.

Everything was against Escalante. Initially the school administration opposed him; the students had little family support. There were no positive role models, and the school had very limited resources. The main thing he had was his own motivation for his students' success. Determined to change the status quo, Escalante had to persuade the first few students who would listen to him that they could control their futures with the right education, and he enrolled them in a newly created calculus class. Ultimately he was able to create a math program that, every year, turned out classes in which almost all the students passed the challenging Advanced Placement Calculus Examination.

The film is a tearjerker and worth seeing. It served our purpose of inspiring and motivating the attendees in our workshop, and it will do the same for you. The message the workshop participants always came away with was: If Escalante could accomplish what he did in circumstances that were many times more difficult than anything I will ever face, then I cannot hide behind the excuse that my environment does not support what I want to accomplish.

BE THE CAUSE IN THE MATTER

The Escalante story is not only about education, just as my experiences in China and at Stanford are not only about teaching. All these stories are about the human experience; they are relevant to all human interactions and all walks of life. They are relevant to your and my family situations, to a mom-and-pop business, to a start-up, and to a large corporation. It does not matter what you do for a living or what your job title is or is not; we all face these same issues of how to get the job done and live a satisfying life.

Being the "cause in the matter" means taking full responsibility for whatever you're dealing with and whatever happens in your life, even when it seems that things are not totally in your control. It's a declaration of choice: instead of playing the role of passive protagonist in your life, choose to take charge of your future. Resolve to get things done, whatever it takes, and no matter how many valid "reasons" pop up.

On a long train ride in China, I noticed that the windows were dirty. I could have complained or sulked about it. Instead I got out during a stop, got a bucket of water, and washed the windows. I decided to be the *cause in the matter* of my trip. If you're missing opportunities because you're waiting for someone else to act, consider how empowering it is to take responsibility for your own experiences.

Even if we have never met, this book has been about you. By telling you my stories, I hope I am motivating you to look at your life in an honest and open way. Underpinning everything is my assumption that you are willing to examine your own experiences and make desired corrections to your future story.

This book has offered many tools and concepts. They can only be of value to you if you are willing to give them a chance. Do not prejudge them. It does not matter if you think they are great or not. What matters is whether they prove to be valuable in your life. Adopt an attitude of willingness to give things a chance; allow yourself to test things out and see what happens without thinking you know the outcome. To test things, you need to give them your attention.

Attention begins with noticing your behaviors and interactions. Notice both yourself and the people you interact with. What works and what doesn't? What could work better? Then test the various tools and exercises in this book by inserting them into your everyday interactions. You can do one of them to start; then add another.

For example, notice how you and your friends use reasons. Then cut back on your use of reasons. Just say what you have to say without justifying it. Modify your way of speaking until you are practically reason-free.

Next, notice how much of what you think and say is clearly a projection. Check yourself on projections. You do this by reversing subject and object in your thoughts or speech. Be aware of which version feels closer to the truth.

The projection exercise will not work if you are not honest with yourself. When one of my students told me that the projection exercises did not work for him, I asked him for an example. He told me that reversing the following sentence did not work: "I am listening to this boring speaker. He goes on and on and does not say anything." I asked him to change subject and object. He came up with "He is listening to my boring talk. I go on and on and do not say anything."

I asked the student if the reversal felt like it had some truth in it. He said no. There was an almost audible sound from the restrained smirks in the class; the other students could not have imagined he would say no. The projection seemed 100 percent accurate to all of us. This student regularly came to class ill-prepared, and to fake it he would ramble on and on, repeating the same inane comments until I found a way to finally interrupt him. Clearly he was not willing to tell himself the truth when he looked at the sentence reversal. It described his behavior perfectly. After I worked with him for a while, he smiled and admitted there might be something for him to think about in the projection exercise.

Unfortunately, I will not be with you to assist you in being honest with yourself. You will need to do it for yourself. Believe me, the projection exercise works. If it does not work for you, chances are you are not willing to look at your truth. Attempt various slight variations in the wording. If it still does not work, imagine me standing behind you, saying, "Tell yourself the truth." If that still does not work, imagine me standing behind you shouting, "Bullshit!"

After you get the hang of noticing your use of reasons and projections, move on to reducing the number of times you say *but* and start using *and* instead. Then move to some of the other exercises in this book.

Informed by your insights and clear intentions, you can use the tools in this book to modify your behavior. Eventually you will think you are getting perfect. That's when you need to start looking at the exercises all over again. Go back to square one and keep fixing yourself. It will keep you busy until you die. It is best to think of the material in this book as a tonic that you need to keep taking, or at least as a seasonal dose—much like an annual flu shot. One shot will not inoculate you for life.

I speak from personal experience.

I was on sabbatical leave in Sweden. During the day, I was leading workshops on creativity and problem solving, using many of the techniques described in this book. At night I was losing sleep, worrying about whether I should retire because I was about to reach what was then the normal retirement age. In the middle of one of the sessions I realized I had not applied what I was teaching to my own problem.

That evening, I asked myself, What would it do for me if I retired?

The answer was: I could stop worrying about whether I should retire. In a flash I realized I had spent six months thinking about the wrong problem. I now had the real question: How do I stop worrying about whether to retire? The answer was obvious: Stop thinking about it. Now, over fifteen years later, I can tell you that since that evening I have never once thought about retiring.

I feel really stupid that I wasted six months on something I did not really care about, and that I was doing it while I was teaching others how to deal with the right question.

Be smarter than I was. Realize that your mind is trickier than you think, and is always working with your ego to make you believe you are doing better than you really are. That's the human condition. What you have going for yourself is that, if you choose to, you can be mindful about controlling both your intentions and your attention to make your life better for yourself and for those around you. You can choose to be the *cause in the matter* of the circumstances of your life and you can instill in yourself the habit of achievement for a more functional and satisfying life.

I hope this book contributes to these worthy goals.

ACKNOWLEDGMENTS

Writing this book turned out to be an unexpected pleasure. The material has been a big part of my life for many years, however, only in the last few years have I felt the desire to share these ideas with a wider audience. This material has been generated over many years, and I am sure that all the sources and influences that led to this book will not be properly remembered or credited. At any rate, here is the way I remember the main threads that led to this book.

At Stanford University one of my first friends was my colleague Bob McKim. Bob had a connection to Mike Murphy, a Stanford graduate and a founder of the Esalen Institute at Big Sur. Mike invited Bob to organize a group of Stanford faculty for a weekend of sampler workshops at Esalen, and I got included. This was my first hands-on introduction to the human potential movement. Out of that experience an Esalen at Stanford program was formed that consisted of weekend workshops on the Stanford campus led by people from Esalen.

At the Esalen weekend I had met Doug Wilde, a popular chemical engineering professor. He and his wife, Jane, were faculty residents at one of the Stanford dorms. Doug invited me to become a faculty affiliate at his dorm. Moreover, he suggested we coteach a class in the dorm under the title "People Dynamics Lab." This would be an experiential one-unit "lab" class built around the Esalen at Stanford program. Students in the class would be required to attend a few of the weekend programs, and the class sessions would be follow-ups to those experiences.

Once we started to teach the class, I attended a large number of the weekend workshops. I had a natural affinity for the material and soon could lead classes without reliance on the Esalen at Stanford program, which ended after a few years. Bob McKim and Doug Wilde are the first people I want to thank; the chances are that without their friendship and initiative, this book would not exist. Although most of them are no longer alive, I do want to thank Fritz Perls, Will Schutz, and other Esalen workshop leaders from whom I learned the craft both at Esalen and during those Stanford weekends. I also want to thank John O. Stevens for writing the book that is a treasure trove of the exercises used in the Esalen workshops, which was of great assistance to me in the beginning of my workshop leadership journey.

After some years I created a graduate version of the "People Dynamics Lab" class. My memory is vague on the transition, and the story I tell is that my friend Jim Fadiman told me that I was schizophrenic and needed to choose among my commitments to engineering, human potential, and politics. Even though Jim is a psychologist, I told him he was wrong and that all three interests were simply alternate expressions of my personality; furthermore, I would show him he was wrong by creating a course that combined all three. I called the course "The Individual and Technology." Jim does not remember, and I am not sure this is the way it really happened; still, I want to thank Jim for many years of friendship and collegiality.

Several years later I renamed the course "The Designer in Society." I thank all the students who participated in the course, regardless of its name. Some have become good friends; others I run into on rare occasions. To all, I am very grateful when you tell me that you remember some experience from the course that has over the years been a treasure in your life. Those meetings have touched me to my core and been a major inspiration to me while writing this book.

I am also thankful to Bob McKim for another important thread: he introduced me to the est workshops and to the est organization's founder, Werner Erhard. I learned a lot from Werner and his work. For me it put an intellectual framework around all the fragments I had gotten from Esalen. I also benefited from coleading several workshops with Werner and his associates. Three years ago I participated in a leadership workshop colead by Werner, Michael Jensen, and Kari Granger. It had been twenty-two years since I last worked with Werner. This experience brought a renewed realization as to how deeply his style and content have influenced my teaching. I am very thankful for his teachings and friendship.

Lynn Johnston has been more than a literary agent, assisting to reshape a rambling manuscript into a work with a distinct point of view. Without her this book would have been published in a much less focused form. She brought professionalism and passion to this project, and I owe her a deep debt of gratitude for her commitment and expertise. She has been a joy to work with.

Jenna Glatzer, my developmental editor, has also been a joy to work with. I will always be thankful that I had access to her expert guidance and professional skills. In spite of a very busy schedule, she generously found the time to give me much-needed guidance. Her thoughtful contributions appear throughout the book.

I thank my faculty colleagues at the Stanford Design Group for many years of collegiality that have provided me with a supportive environment for my work. I want to especially thank Sheri Sheppard, for taking the time to read two early drafts of the first chapters of this manuscript. Special thanks to Dave Kelley for inviting me to take part in the creation of the d.school and for permission to use the iconic mind map he created at the beginning of our d.school journey.

In the d.school I have been blessed with colleagues who read my manuscript and provided structural suggestions that were extremely helpful (even when they were in complete contradiction to each other!). In this regard I thank Thomas Both, Scott Doorley, Perry Klebahn, Adam Royalty, and Jeremy Utley. Emi Kolawole went beyond the call of duty and provided extensive language edits that have made this a more readable book; I owe her much. Caitria O'Neill generously connected me with a publishing contact. I also want to thank Sarah Stein Greenberg for her strong support of my book writing project.

I want to again mention Thomas Both, and thank him for his extraordinary work in creating the illustrations and front cover concepts on very short notice. Although I had his support throughout the project, this new role put demands on his talents and time that went beyond what was reasonable. He has my profound thanks for having so willingly joined me in my hour of need.

Starting with a prototype from the publisher, Thomas Both created alternative front covers. In developing the cover designs he involved Scoot Doorley, Charlotte Burgess Auburn, and Stacey Gray as his principal consultants. In addition he received valuable advice from Justin Ferrell, Chris Flink, Ashish Goel, Mark Grundberg, Seamus Harte, Emi Kolawole, Danielle Kraus, and Erik Olesund. I am very thankful to everyone who assisted.

Bill Scott created drafts for illustrations and a cover and advised on aesthetic considerations for the first draft of the manuscript. He and his dog were the source of much pleasure to me and Ruth during our meetings. In spite of a busy schedule he generously took time to donate his talent and insights to this project, and for that I am grateful.

Haakon Faste went to considerable effort to produce a cleaned-up copy of Rolf Faste's drawing. I thank him for his efforts and his permission to use his father's drawing.

Ann Davidson, Elliot Roth, Marcia Ruotolo, and Donalda Speight were kind enough to read the entire manuscript and provide detailed structural and language edits. Also my wife, Ruth Roth, and her book club provided useful editorial suggestions.

I am also very thankful for the early encouragement and guidance I received from R. B. Brenner. I am grateful to Paddy Hirsh for introducing me to his agent, and to Barry Katz, Tina Seelig, and Doug Wilde for generously introducing me to their editors. I am eternally grateful to Raju Narisetti for introducing me to Lynn Johnston. Jim Adams, Tom Kosnick, Douglas Sery, Bob Sutton, and Kate Wahl shared their ideas about routes to publication.

At HarperCollins, I thank my editor, Colleen Lawrie, for

her support of this project and her expert editing and guidance. And I also thank Miranda Ottewell for her thoughtful and thorough line editing.

I especially want to thank my family and all the friends and colleagues mentioned in this book. To all of you, I am grateful for our interactions, which have provided me with the material for this book and been the bedrock of a rich and fulfilling life.

NOTES

INTRODUCTION: YELLOW-EYED CATS

1. The course's original title was "The Individual and Technology." Four years later I revised it and renamed it "The Designer in Society." Neither title is an adequate description of the course content.
2. "Forget B-School: D-School Is Hot," *Wall Street Journal*, Jan. 7, 2012.
3. For example, Tim Brown, *Change by Design* (New York: Harper-Collins, 2009).
4. Snell Putney and Gail J. Putney, *The Adjusted American: Normal Neuroses in the Individual and Society* (New York: Harper & Row, 1964).
5. Another version of the design thinking process uses *understand* and *observe* instead of *empathy*. The *define* part of the process is often labeled "point of view" (POV). In this case the process is: understand, observe, POV, ideate, prototype, test.

CHAPTER 1: NOTHING IS WHAT YOU THINK IT IS

1. People are more concerned with their self-image than with their actions. See experiments reported in Christopher J. Bryan, Gabrielle S. Adams, and Benoît Monin, "When Cheating Would Make You a Cheater: Implicating the Self Prevents Unethical Behavior," *Journal of Experimental Psychology: General* 142, no. 4 (2013): 1001–5.
2. Carol Dweck, *Mindset: The New Psychology of Success* (New York: Random House, 2006), p. 6, emphasis in original.

3. The film *Professor Poubelle* can be found on YouTube.
4. Self-efficacy is discussed in many publications by Albert Bandura and his coworkers. See especially Bandura, *Self-Efficacy: The Exercise of Control* (New York: W. H. Freeman, 1997).
5. Kenneth P. Oakley, "Skill as a Human Possession," in *A History of Technology*, ed. Charles Singer, E. J. Holmyard, and A. R. Hall (New York: Charles Scribner's Sons, 1954), 1: 2–3.
6. Dr. Rudy Tanzi recommends these steps in his television series *Super Brain*. Also see his book coauthored with Deepak Chopra: Deepak Chopra and Rudolf E. Tanzi, *Super Brain* (New York: Harmony Books, 2012).

CHAPTER 2: REASONS ARE BULLSHIT

1. Eric Hoffer, in *The Passionate State of Mind and Other Aphorisms* (New York: Harper & Brothers, 1955), says it best in his aphorism no. 70: "We lie loudest when we lie to ourselves."

CHAPTER 3: GETTING UNSTUCK

Epigraph: This was a favorite saying of Rolf Faste's, derived by turning the usual platitude about doing things on its head. To me it is the perfect caution against charging ahead when you have mistaken an answer for a question.

1. There are several variations for defining a POV. One of the most common calls for a phrase describing a specific user followed by a phrase specifying a need and finally a phrase giving an insight to what (not how!) the solution needs to accomplish. An example of a POV statement is: A poor single mother needs financial know-how so she can learn to use her money efficiently.
2. See, for example, Vijay Kumar, *101 Design Methods* (New York: John Wiley & Sons, 2013).
3. Hamilton later wrote to his son describing the history of his discovery: "Your mother was walking with me, along the Royal Canal, to which she had perhaps driven; and although she talked with me now and then, yet an *under-current* of thought was going on in my mind, which gave at last a *result*, whereof it is not too much to say that I felt *at once* the importance." Quote taken from a letter dated August 5, 1865, reprinted in Robert P. Graves's biography of Hamilton.
4. The idea of checklist solitaire seems to have come from John E. Arnold, a professor at MIT and Stanford. He actually had card decks made with graphic illustrations of each transformation. They were hand-drawn and

used in his classes and consulting practice. There seems not to have been any commercial production of these, however.

5. S. I. Hayakawa and A. R. Hayakawa, *Language in Thought and Action* (San Diego: Harcourt, 1991).

CHAPTER 5: DOING IS EVERYTHING

1. Experimental verification is difficult when the results do not fit into existing paradigms. See, for example, Henry M. Collins and Trevor Pinch, *The Golem: What You Should Know About Science*, 2nd ed. (New York: Cambridge University Press, 2012), which presents several case studies in which the perceived efficacy of experimental studies strongly depended on whether they matched the existing paradigm. Collins and Pinch discuss some famous experiments that were defective in proving what was claimed yet were accepted because they were in accord with current beliefs, and some that were rejected because they did not fit into the then current belief system.

CHAPTER 6: WATCH YOUR LANGUAGE

1. The original meaning relies on the fact that *proves* meant "tests," not "confirms." So it actually implies that an exception (i.e., a single counterexample) is enough to disprove the rule. I choose to use the interpretation where *proves* means "confirms."

2. Actors know that in addition to what they say, how they behave (i.e., body language) is very important. In an interview on the PBS program *Charlie Rose*, Academy Award–winning actor Dustin Hoffman described his frustrations in mastering the characters in such difficult roles as the crippled street hustler in *Midnight Cowboy*, the autistic brother in *Rain Man*, and an actor pretending to be a woman in *Tootsie*. He was blocked in each case to the point of wanting to withdraw from the part, and then he had a breakthrough thanks to seeing someone who inspired the behavior he wanted to portray.

3. Thomas Gordon was an American clinical psychologist and colleague of Carl Rogers. He is widely recognized as a pioneer in teaching communication skills and conflict resolution methods. The model he developed came to be known as the Gordon model or the Gordon method, a communication style for building and maintaining effective relationships.

CHAPTER 7: GROUP HABITS

Epigraph: This is from an actual conversation I had. It took place long before Facebook, Twitter, and other social media existed. The irony between

Harold's attitudes and those of the current social media–addicted generation should be obvious. Temperamentally, I am with Harold: I really don't want strangers (and most friends) to know "my business."

1. My colleague Professor Douglass Wilde advocates using personality type to compose teams. He has written three books describing his methods, the latest being *Teamology: The Construction and Organization of Effective Teams* (London: Springer-Verlag, 2009).

2. For more about Synectics, see Gordon, *Synectics* (New York: Harper, 1961), and George M. Prince, *The Practice of Creativity* (New York: Collier, 1970).

3. By 2005 the Mechanical Engineering Department had grown from three to five divisions. Then the department chair decided that the word *division* was too divisive, and the names of all the department's divisions were changed to replace the word *division* with *group*, so the Design Division is now called the Design Group.

4. An in-depth treatment of the negative side of using competition as a motivator is given in Alfie Kohn, *No Contest: The Case Against Competition* (Boston: Houghton Mifflin, 1986).

CHAPTER 8: SELF-IMAGE BY DESIGN

Epigraph: This appears in many variants from many sources. Its use here is not meant to discourage taking chances and making mistakes; it is meant instead to remind one about the sin of arrogance.

1. A detailed analysis of life's stages related to the social forces leading to marriage can be found in Gail Putney Fullerton, *Survival in Marriage* (New York: Holt, Rinehart and Winston, 1972).

2. Argyris is the James B. Conant Professor at the Harvard Graduate Schools of Business and Education. The quote is from his article "Teaching Smart People How to Learn," *Harvard Business Review*, May 1991, p. 103.

3. On boosting creative confidence, see Tom Kelley and David Kelley, *Creative Confidence: Unleashing the Creative Potential Within Us All* (New York: Crown Business, 2013).

4. The Truth Process uses guided imagery and is related to other self-awareness methods including those used in gestalt therapy, primal scream therapy, mind dynamics, the Silva Method, and the auditing practice in Scientology.

CHAPTER 9: THE BIG PICTURE

Epigraph: This Nietzsche quote is used as the prologue for the text in Putney and Putney, *The Adjusted American*. In using it I have two purposes.

First, it is my homage to *The Adjusted American* for providing the first motivation for this book. Second, I like that it implies that it is normal for people to have a sane life even though we live in a crazy world.

1.   Kurt Vonnegut, *Player Piano* (New York: Doubleday, 1952).
2.   Harry Braverman, *Labor and Monopoly Capital* (New York: Monthly Review Press, 1974).
3.   Gandhi is quoted as having said this in Delhi in 1924 by Mahadev DeSai; cited in the preface to Mahatma Gandhi, *Hind Swaraj or Indian Home Rule* (Ahmedabad, India: Jitendra T. Desai/Navajivan, 1938), pp. 5–6.
4.   E. F. Schumacher, *Small Is Beautiful: Economics as if People Mattered* (New York: HarperCollins, 1973).
5.   Ibid., pp. 56-66.
6.   Lawrence Weschler, *Seeing Is Forgetting the Name of the Thing One Sees* (Berkeley: University of California Press, 1982).
7.   The quest for personal autonomy in a harsh assembly line environment is insightfully portrayed in the short story "Joe, the Vanishing American" by Harvey Swados (1957). This and fifty-four other classic writings dealing with the relationship between people and machines are republished in the anthology, edited by Arthur O. Lewis Jr., *Of Men and Machines* (New York: E. P. Dutton, 1963).
8.   From Lewis Wirth's preface to Karl Mannheim's *Ideology and Utopia* (New York: Harcourt Brace, 1936), p. xxiv.

CHAPTER 10: MAKE ACHIEVEMENT YOUR HABIT
Epigraph: Rolf Faste used a variant that I prefer: "Hardening of the categories leads to art failure."

BIBLIOGRAPHY

Adams, J. L. *Conceptual Blockbusting.* 4th ed. Cambridge, MA: Perseus, 2001.

Argyris, Chris. "Teaching Smart People How to Learn." *Harvard Business Review*, May 1991, pp. 99–109.

Bandura, Albert. *Self-Efficacy: The Exercise of Control.* New York: W. H. Freeman, 1997.

Braverman, Harry. *Labor and Monopoly Capital.* New York: Monthly Review Press, 1974.

Brown, Tim. *Change by Design: How Design Thinking Transforms Organizations and Inspires Innovation.* New York: HarperCollins, 2009.

Bryan, Christopher J., Gabrielle S. Adams, and Benoît Monin. "When Cheating Would Make You a Cheater: Implicating the Self Prevents Unethical Behavior." *Journal of Experimental Psychology: General* 142, no. 4 (2013): pp. 1001–5.

Chopra, Deepak, and Rudolph E. Tanzi. *Super Brain: Unleashing the Explosive Power of Your Mind to Maximize Health, Happiness, and Spiritual Well-Being.* New York: Harmony Books, 2012.

Collins, Henry M., and Trevor Pinch. *The Golem: What You Should Know About Science.* 2nd ed. New York: Cambridge University Press, 2012.

Davidson, Ann. *Alzheimer's, a Love Story: One Year in My Husband's Journey.* Secaucus, NJ: Birch Lane, 1997.

———. *A Curious Kind of Widow.* McKinleyville, CA: Fithian, 2006.

———. "Modified Radical." *New England Journal of Medicine* 321, no. 9 (1989): 619.

———. *Modified Radical and Other Cancer Poems.* Palo Alto, CA: Monday Press, 1990.

Doorley, Scott, and Scott Witthoft. *Make Space.* Hoboken, NJ: John Wiley & Sons, 2012.

Dweck, Carol. *Mindset: The New Psychology of Success.* New York: Random House, 2006.

Fullerton, Gail Putney. *Survival in Marriage.* New York: Holt, Rinehart and Winston, 1972.

Gandhi, Mahatma. *Hind Swaraj or Indian Home Rule.* Ahmedabad, India: Jitendra T. Desai/Navajivan, 1938.

Goncharov, Ivan. *Oblomov.* Translated by David Magarshack. 1859. Reprint. London: Penguin, 1954.

Gordon, William J. J. *Synectics: The Development of Creative Capacity.* New York: Harper, 1961.

Graves, Robert P. *Life of Sir William Rowan Hamilton.* Volume II, Chapter XXVIII. Dublin: Dublin University Press, 1885.

Hayakawa, S. I., and A. R. Hayakawa. *Language in Thought and Action.* 5th ed. San Diego: Harcourt, 1991.

Hoffer, Eric. *The Passionate State of Mind and Other Aphorisms.* New York: Harper & Brothers, 1955.

Kahneman, Daniel. *Thinking, Fast and Slow.* New York: Random House, 2011.

Kelley, Tom, and David Kelley. *Creative Confidence: Unleashing the Creative Potential Within Us All.* New York: Crown Business, 2013.

Kohn, Alfie. *No Contest: The Case Against Competition.* Boston: Houghton Mifflin, 1986.

Kumar, Vijay. *101 Design Methods.* New York: John Wiley & Sons, 2013.

Lewis, Arthur O. Jr., ed. *Of Men and Machines.* New York: E. P. Dutton, 1963.

Maltz, Maxwell. *Psycho-Cybernetics.* New York: Pocket Books, 1960.

Mannheim, Karl. *Ideology and Utopia.* New York: Harcourt, Brace, 1936.

Oakley, Kenneth P. "Skill as a Human Possession." In *A History of Technology,* ed. Charles Singer, E. J. Holmyard, and A. R. Hall, 1: 2–3. New York: Charles Scribner's Sons, 1954.

Prince, George M. *The Practice of Creativity.* New York: Collier, 1970.

Putney, Snell, and Gail J. Putney. *The Adjusted American: Normal Neuroses in the Individual and Society.* New York: Harper & Row, 1964.

Schumacher, E. F. *Small Is Beautiful: Economics as if People Mattered.* New York: HarperCollins, 1973.

Stevens, John O. *Awareness: Exploring, Experimenting, Experiencing.* Lafayette, CA: Real People Press, 1971.

Steinbeck, John. *The Grapes of Wrath.* New York: Viking, 1939.

Swados, Harvey. "Joe, the Vanishing American." *Hudson Review* 10, no. 2 (1957): 201–18.

Vonnegut, Kurt. *Player Piano.* New York: Doubleday, 1952.

Weschler, Lawrence. *Seeing Is Forgetting the Name of the Thing One Sees.* Berkeley: University of California Press, 1982.

Wilde, Douglass. *Teamology: The Construction and Organization of Effective Teams.* London: Springer-Verlag, 2009.

ABOUT THE AUTHOR

Bernard Roth is the Rodney H. Adams Professor of Engineering and the academic director of the Hasso Plattner Institute of Design (the d.school) at Stanford University. He is a leading expert in kinematics, the science of motion, and one of the world's pioneers in the area of robotics. In addition, he has created courses that allow students to directly gain understanding and experience about personal issues that matter to them. Bernie is also the primary developer of the concept of the Creativity Workshop. For more than thirty years this workshop has been a vehicle for him to take the experiential teaching he developed at Stanford to students, faculty, and professionals around the world. He is an in-demand speaker at conferences and workshops globally, has served as a director of several corporations, and has been a leader in professional societies.